T0196049

BACK OF THE NAPKIN

A Start-Up's Legal Path from Idea to Enterprise

ALICIA LOCHEED GOODROW

ARCHWAY
PUBLISHING

Archway Publishing books may be ordered through booksellers or by contacting:

Archway Publishing
1663 Liberty Drive
Bloomington, IN 47403
www.archwaypublishing.com
844-669-3957

ISBN: 978-1-6657-1344-3 (sc)
ISBN: 978-1-6657-1345-0 (e)

Library of Congress Control Number: 2021920511

Print information available on the last page.

Archway Publishing rev. date: 11/03/2021

CONTENTS

ACKNOWLEDGMENTS

This book is thirty years overdue. I started it in 1991 when Ken Simon tapped me to give a seminar on choice of entity in front of a group of experienced lawyers and business leaders. I was twenty-five years old. Over the years, my clients have been my muse, challenging me to develop simple tools to explain complicated concepts and homework to help them focus their priorities. I created many parts of this book on the back of a napkin while listening to excited founders trust me with their big ideas.

My patient husband, Henry, and now young adult kids, Haley, and Zach, know more about LLCs than most people and perhaps more than some lawyers. They supported me when I followed my crazy dreams, from the big idea of a film production company to writing a book during COVID quarantine. The Founders' Team of Pantheon of Women (Donna Cole, Deborah Kainer, and others) taught me what is like to be on the business side of the table with a big idea, hoping to build an enterprise.

My law partners (present and past) also have cheered me on—especially Cliff Simpson, who has shared a thin office wall with me for many years and hears all my wild ideas before most people. Beth Fulkerson and Michael Dunnam went a step further, contributing most of the content for chapter 9 and the accompanying homework. Both Beth and Michael are great teachers who believe in empowering clients by teaching legal principles. Brent Somers contributed the lease checklist and read drafts of other chapters. The flexibility and encouragement afforded by the community of partners at Culhane Meadows made this work possible in many ways.

My creative interns, Shayla Zamorah, Maggie Erwin, and Haley Wilkerson, helped me focus and speak with clarity as a teacher and not just a lawyer.

For all of these contributions and the many more gifts I have received, I am thankful.

PREFACE

The law is a tool. It is a means to an end—not an end in itself. Contracts should help you accomplish your goals and are only useful if you understand them and use them properly. Contracts are ultimately about documenting the trust and commitments you have in relationships you build as you build your company.

I have advised private companies, including start-ups, for thirty years. Most companies either avoid lawyers altogether for the first several months/years because they think they are expensive, or they waste money on legal fees that do not accomplish their goals. Lawyers are useful and add value as counselors, tax advisers, coaches, and risk managers. But you have to do your homework and communicate your goals clearly, or you'll waste time and money.

This book is your homework. If you work through it, you will be prepared to use the law as a tool to protect you, prepare you, and lay a strong foundation for your company's growth. You will still need a lawyer, but you will be prepared to work as a teammate with your lawyer to accomplish your business goals. Once you and your team do the homework, you and your lawyers can document your decisions professionally and help you plan for future scenarios without losing your mind, momentum, or money.

THE HUMAN FACTOR

You and your cofounders have scribbled your great idea on the back of the napkin. Maybe you've had several meetings to translate this into a preliminary business plan. Perhaps you've even scrounged up some preliminary commitments of funding or started spending some of your savings or run up some credit card bills on your great idea. But you may be neglecting the greatest risk facing all new companies: the Human Factor.

All contracts are built on relationships—not form documents and not handshakes. If you start with a form document, the form will shape your relationships—not vice versa. If you start with a handshake, you will never really know where you stand with the other side. Take the time now—at the beginning—to figure out, as a team, where you stand and to clarify in writing the expectations and roles of each player.

Experienced business leaders have a solid and honest understanding of all key relationships that underly their business.

The relationships you have with founders, investors, customers, suppliers, contractors, and employees not only can but ultimately will make or break the company.

Reading the histories of famous entrepreneurs from Tesla and Westinghouse to Bill Gates and Mark Zuckerberg, one finds that the success or failure of understanding and putting solid legal and emotional frameworks around key relationships was a critical factor. Deferred maintenance around relationships—pushing messy issues and conflicts aside for later resolution—is often a very costly decision and in some cases has led to the failure of the company.

This book is about the process of sorting out the people side of things up front. It will save you time, money, and headaches in the present and future. Legal agreements follow human relationships. Once you've successfully sorted out the humans, the contracts can protect you.

There are five kinds of core relationships:

- founders
- people with money to invest
- customers
- suppliers
- Key Contributors of time and talent

Depending on the type of business, you'll address your relationships with each of these groups in different orders and with different types of legal tools. But ultimately you must document your agreements with each of them.

Relationships are not static. And contracts don't have to be static either. In many cases, it is better to make your best guess and put a good but not great contract in place instead of ignoring the issue and working under a handshake.

Upgrade to better contracts when you have some real value to protect.

Upgrade to better or different contracts when your relationships change—and they will change radically over time.

To help you understand the Human Factor in all contracts more clearly, we're introducing you to four core character stories. You will find yourself, your cofounders, your investors, your advisers, and your other key players among the humans in these stories. Use them as case studies to help you understand the goals of the homework. Use them to help start meaningful dialogues about the important but tough conversations you must have to build the legal scaffolding to take you from idea to enterprise.

CORE CHARACTER STORIES

Meet the Humans and Their Stories

Now, let's meet some of the humans we'll be referencing in this book. Their relationships will shape their business decisions and inform how their businesses are driven. Sorting out the Human Factor can seem unnecessary, but it's the most important part. You will meet everyone from two entrepreneurial women with adult children who are looking to sell their great idea, to rocket engineers just starting out after graduate school. Who do they remind you of? And why? Which character do you identify with most? Ask yourself these questions as you read. Which business do you feel mirrors yours? Is there anything you would want to ask the characters if you could? Think about your own friends and family and business partners; these relationships are important. The Human Factor means more than just being a charismatic businessperson. It means building on the base you have, sorting out the tough stuff, and allowing your relationships with others to shape your business and legal model, not the other way around. The following stories will guide you through each of the lessons in this book, serving as a reminder to never forget the humans.

Disclaimer: The characters and stories in this book are fictional. Any resemblance to actual humans is merely coincidental. None of the interactions between the fictional characters and companies and any real companies represent any real business transactions. All legal relationships and contracts are for illustration purposes only and should not be taken as legal advice applicable to your specific company or personal legal situation.

Camp Cars. Alicia and Michelle are opening an alternative car rental business in Utah or Arizona. They intend to target a niche, underserved market of vacationers traveling by RV with the goal of building the company for sale to a larger, national enterprise such as Zip Car. They intend to develop up to five proof of concept loca- tions over three years, then search for a buyer either in private equity or a competitor. Ideally, they would join a chain of alternative car rentals in nontraditional locations.

Several alternative car rental models exist. Some own and manage a fleet of cars available for hourly rental in dense urban areas or university campuses. Others function as a platform for private persons to lease their underused cars to people needing a rental car. Alicia and Michelle think the fleet ownership model will be best for them, and they hope to partner with a major car manufacturer in a joint venture for the initial project. Alicia worked for a major car manufacturer in a prior career and knows they are very supportive of women-owned businesses.

For people in nontraditional locations who need access to a vehicle, Alicia and Michelle's company (for now called Camp Cars) provides a reliable source of transportation. As they expand, they could also offer four-by-fours or motorcycles for use in national parks or BLM lands. Their working name for the company is Park Car, evoking images of fun motorcycle adventures on Route 66.

They have a budget of $600,000, including the purchase of five vehicles, seasonal employees, and a concession fee budget for two large RV parks. In the beginning, Alicia and Michelle will rely considerably on friends, fools, and family (which you will learn about later in this book) for talent, advice, and maybe some money. They will need to have a solid and successful business plan in order to do so. If they are able to negotiate a joint venture with a major brand, they could expand quickly but may have to give up significant ownership.

Both Alicia and Michelle are single parents with young adult children who need summer jobs. And they plan to keep their own day jobs while perhaps working remotely to get the business set up. So, phase 1 will be a true bootstrap operation.

Rocket Fuel. Luke and Marco and Sally are launching a rocket fuel company based on collaborative lab research they did at Rice University last summer in their postgrad programs with Rice and NASA.

Luke, Marco, and Sally all share a similar trait: their passion for scientific progress and impressive aptitude for physics and engineering. Luke is the technical one, the driving force behind the engineering. Sally is the people person, always meeting with top faculty members at Rice to earn their praise. Marco is an international student on a student visa and an impressive engineer as well. He is the business visionary. They were finalists in the Rice Business Plan Competition and as a result received some substantial initial funding. They are launching a rocket fuel company called Rocket Fuel, which emerged from a research project they all worked on through a joint program with Rice University and NASA. Their dreams for their company are not necessarily to develop a national chain but rather to provide top-notch engineering for the progression of space exploration. As close colleagues, they envision a collaborative business model in which they can each pursue their niche while ultimately driving the business forward. Company Rocket Fuel is targeting the growing market of private rocket-launching companies in and around Houston.

Rice University owns an interest in all intellectual property developed by its students and professors. So, this team will have a cofounder/partner from the very start that sets certain expectations and possibly provides resources beyond what a traditional start-up could expect. Ideally, this cofounder will have an established background in intellectual property rights, so they are well equipped to deal with the complex issues surrounding higher education property ownership.

There are grants and funding sources available for research like this. Their initial launch budget is only $250,000, but they expect to need more than $5,000,000 in the first two years from various sources. The Rice Business Plan Competition award money Luke, Marco, and Sally received will give them a considerable advantage as well.

Their exit strategy is to sell to a company like SpaceX in three to five years. One of the founders of Space X toured Rice University last year and met Luke, Marco, and Sally and complimented them on their work.

Law Firm. Maggie, Shayla, and Jorge are launching a women/minority-owned law firm in Houston, hoping to do business with the renewable energy business.

Maggie, Shayla, and Jorge graduated from the University of Houston Law Center with the dream of building a minority-owned law firm in the Houston area. All three have worked for several years in large law firms, working for Houston's major energy companies, and they have saved up some money on the side. They have all established relationships with strong mentors in the field, a possible advisory board for the future. Maggie and Shayla are both in their thirties, married but without kids. Jorge has one special needs child and is not married. They met through a study group while in law school and have been close business colleagues ever since.

They hope to focus on the renewable energy business because they believe that the future of all business enterprises will focus on being greener. It is unclear whether private renewable energy companies will look at minority- and women-owned law firms with any kind of preference, but they know that the majors have institutional minority-hiring programs in place.

They plan on using their personal savings to fund their law firm. To help save money, they are looking into the possibility of creating a virtual law firm in order to work from home to save the costs of office maintenance and other expenses. Once they get up and running, they might look into hiring staff, but for now, they want to take on all of the work themselves.

All three have strong mentors inside and outside of their existing law firm employers. They are nervous about burning bridges but understand the need to set their own course at this second phase of their careers.

Diamond Productions. Christine, Elara, and Tomas are launching a film production company—indie films at first, but it may grow larger.

As filmmakers with more than twenty-five years of experience, Christine, Elara, and Tomas want to help other artists achieve their dreams by nurturing the filmmaking careers of minority filmmakers. They decided to launch a film production company called Diamond Productions to produce indie films with budgets under $5mm in Cleveland, to take advantage of tax and community credits for opening new businesses in historically blighted areas. They might expand their services eventually, but they're in no rush to grow the business. They can fund up to five films from their own funds but will raise capital through a fund once the first few films get through production. They want to establish a flexible process that's client focused. To simplify the process for their clients, they want to make Diamond Productions a one-stop shop by offering the three stages of video production: preproduction, production, postproduction, and distribution for select films. They have deep relationships with Netflix, Disney, and Hulu. Their hope is to guide the clients from storyboard to the final film and everything in between.

Each one of the founders has had considerable individual success. Christine met Elara on the set of one of the highest-grossing films in the past ten years, and they have been friends ever since. Introduced through a mutual friend to Tomas, Elara and Christine decided she would make an excellent business partner for their new idea. This is a build and hold business for the founders. They have significant personal wealth and solid industry and community reputations, and this is a way to pay it forward for the next generation of filmmakers. They have considered setting up a sidecar foundation or becoming a B corporation to highlight their dual goals of making money and paying it forward.

CHAPTER 1

Building the Founders' Team

You are eager to get started with the launch. You hope to raise capital, find the perfect location, develop the key software, put up a website, register a trademark, enter contracts, quit your day job, and live the dream, building something bigger and better. But first, let's work on building your team. You'll need a large stack of napkins to jot down your progress as you take this first step.

Note that this team-building chapter will require four or more group sessions and time for individual homework. We recommend that you calendar the sessions outside work hours over thirty days or find a way to take a retreat together for two days. If you have experience leading teams, you can follow the path in this chapter without outside assistance. But if you are new to team building or have a group with divergent experience or personalities, you may want to engage an outside coach to help.

This chapter is built around *lessons, Pizza Party prep exercises,* and *pizza parties.*

The Pizza Party prep exercises are necessary to figuring out your specific Human Factors that will profoundly affect the first stage of your company's growth and could be the difference between success, stagnation, and untimely meltdown. Read the lessons. Rally your team into doing the Pizza Party prep exercises, and really commit to honesty and hard work at the pizza parties.

I promise you that these steps are *as important as* or more important than a solid, out-of-the-starting-blocks business plan. If you skip these important steps, you will spend time, money, and sleepless nights and will possibly garner lawsuits sorting out the Human Factors later.

Lesson 1: Who Is at the Founders' Table and Why? Inventory the players and sort them into the right categories: founders, nonequity Key Contributors, investors, and others.

Lesson 2: Get to Know the Founders Really Well. Personal questionnaires and frank conversations are essential to this exercise.

Lesson 3: Identify Your Leadership Paradigm. Honest evaluation of pecking order, expectations of leadership roles, and ultimate decision rights are the goal of this exercise.

Lesson 4: Find the Right Roles for Each Person and Complete Your Decision Matrix.

To walk through these steps, we suggest that you schedule a series of casual evening pizza parties or something similar. You will want about ninety minutes of relaxed time—preferably outside the home or office. Create a safe space for people to be honest and for your team to begin to communicate openly about their goals. These pizza parties focus on *people,* not *product.* This is not the time to work seriously on the business plan, the goals, the name, the money, or other factors. Don't try to squeeze in time to take a quick look at proposed leases or names or any other details. Focus on the individual goals and perspectives of each founder. Focus on building the right team and leadership paradigm—the Human Factor. Set a goal of assigning the proper leadership roles by the end of the series of pizza parties.

If you really dig in on the work of chapter 1, the rest of this book will be much easier because you will have sorted out the Human Factor by creating a strong team of founders who know one another and their respective roles in leadership for the company.

Note that it is possible to do the prep exercises and pizza parties in a weekend retreat format as long as you allow plenty of break time for the individuals to reflect on their answers separately as well as in a group setting.

Remember to get the people right and get the right people, and you will sail through the other hurdles much more smoothly.

 **Lesson 1: Who Is at the Founders' Table and Why?**

They seem like easy questions. But Mark Zuckerberg got the answers wrong (and paid a lot of money in settlement to the Winklevoss brothers), and you might also mess this one up.

If you invite too many people to the Founders' Table, you will never get anything done.

If you forget to invite someone who thinks he or she deserve to be there, you will end up with a grudge match on the good end and a lawsuit on the bad end of the spectrum.

First, before you send out invitations to the first Pizza Party, make a list of people you envision at the table. Those who are splitting the tab on the pitchers of beer and extra-large, extra-topping pies are the obvious candidates. You value each other. You have some idea what your respective roles are. You cannot imagine (right now) proceeding without any of you. And you will take turns grabbing that last slice of pepperoni instead of fighting about it.

Second, list the "invisible" people who may not be given a seat at the table but might imagine that they should be. Maybe they have been eating leftover slices in the breakroom behind the scenes or have been taking out metaphorical empty pizza boxes for some time now and feel like part of the team.

Hint: if you make money, founders will appear out of thin air and want a piece of the action.

Who can you imagine might appear out of nowhere on the eve of your much-anticipated $100 million exit?

Some possible candidates include the following:

- Your college roommate who listened to you dream dreams for two years and gave up his summers to help in the garage with the project. Maybe he or she kept the scribbles on the back of the napkin.
- Your current employer who snuck some "assignment of rights" or "work for hire" language into its employee handbook and effectively owns all your ideas while you're employed.
- Your mom's best friend who gave you "free" advice for two years.
- That geeky kid in your college class who worked with you on the group project where you talked about your great ideas for this company (and she kept the notes).

- That nosey coworker on your last job who listened in on every coffee-bar conversation you had with the people eating pizza today.
- Your spouse (or ex-spouse).

Third, list the people who have put in something of value. We will deal with the investors later, but for now, include anyone who has given you "something for nothing," such as the following:

- free rent
- free software
- free equipment
- free services (e.g., legal, accounting, financial modeling, software/programming, and/or product testing)

Is there anyone on list 2 or list 3 who should be invited to the Founders' Table? If yes, why? If you are on the fence about inviting someone, you might want to read ahead to steps 2–4 to imagine how including the hypothetical founder would play out in forming your team, determining your leadership paradigm, and assigning roles. If you can still imagine the contributor as a founder after working through those exercises, then include him or her in the first Pizza Party and test out the dynamic there.

Can you make anyone you identified in the previous question go away happy now, without giving them equity? Not everyone wants equity. Freebees can go a long way, as we will see later. Also, salaries and payments of cash to independent contractors or suppliers are more valuable than equity to many important people.

For persons in categories 2 and 3, you can structure compensation that may even include equity, but be careful about promising that up front. And you should define their roles clearly. But they don't have to be founders.

One interesting question to ask: can you reasonably replace the skills, energy, or personality and not lose momentum for the company? If the answer is yes, then be very judicious about including them at the Founders' Table.

If you include people from list 2 or list 3 in your pizza parties, you might want to graciously uninvite them now.

Important fact: You want to keep as much equity as you can in a small group for now. While you may sell or give away equity later, keep the core group small.

Law Firm Story

When Maggie, Shayla, and Jorge first sat down to hash out plans for their law firm, they had to sort out who would be a founder and who was of counsel or an employee. Two semiretired partners served as strong mentors from their past work at prestigious law firms. Originally, they considered bringing in these two experienced veterans to give their firm some brand value and take advantage of the experience of the veterans. But after holding their first Pizza Party without the two veteran lawyers, the three agreed it was time to set out on their own path. The advice from their previous relationships was valuable, and they were willing to offer them positions with economic significance, but these folks were not founders. The two senior lawyers helped inspire and organize the new firm, but in the end, the three founders aren't sharing that last pizza slice with the two veterans.

Rocket Fuel Story

When the original founders of Rocket Fuel met for their first Pizza Party, they included two other people: Professor Smart and Ms. Money. Professor Smart had been the team's key academic adviser for several years and had been influential in their decision to take the project to the Rice Business Plan Competition. They relied on his advice on technical and business issues. Ms. Money had been on the jury panel for the competition and offered to become a lead investor. Both Professor Smart and Ms. Money have other jobs and support several start-up companies. They have experience and strong opinions. But it was unclear whether either had the commitment or interest in taking on the daily sacrifices necessary to get the company going. The three founders met separately after the first Pizza Party and decided that they might offer equity to both Ms. Money and Professor Smart when they raised their first round and that they might be willing to negotiate roles for them as consultants, but the group dynamic of three felt better. Without the exercise of the Pizza Party, they would have automatically included the two advisers in the founders' group.

Pizza Party 1—Who Is at the Founders' Table and Why?

In this lesson, the initial founders at the Pizza Party will focus on building consensus around the big-picture goals for the company, the hypothetical endgame and timeline, and a high-level view of each person's commitment and role. Then you will begin to look at whether you have the right assemblage of talents and personalities. There are multiple Pizza Party prep exercises for this Pizza Party.

Pizza Party

Schedule a ninety-minute meeting with the people you think should be part of the project for the long run (the Founders' Table). Order pizza and maybe a six-pack or two (you really shouldn't have more than six people). Try to make it an electronics-free zone for a couple of hours so you can really focus. If possible, hold the event away from everyone's home turf; it doesn't work as well by video conference, in someone's home, or in an office. You want everyone to be equally comfortable and uncomfortable.

After you schedule the party but before it starts:

- Ask yourself the questions in Pizza Party Prep 1 on behalf of yourself and each founder.

- If you are not experienced at leading groups, consider hiring a coach or at least reading up on some of the excellent business-focused literature on communications and team building.

At the Pizza Party

Set a relaxed tone and build early consensus by successfully ordering shared dinner. Seriously, work to agree on a type of pizza or another shared/common meal. It will help you see how the different people communicate. Which ones are deferential? Who takes charge? Who listens carefully to the preferences of others? It is OK to have one strong leader or a couple or three of them. It is important to know how you interact together.

Watch eye contact and body language.

Take your own notes and review them before the next meeting.

Work on the Key Players Pizza Party 1 Prep 1. Talk about which of you will play the different roles usually required to grow and operate a successful company and then move on to Pizza Party 1 Prep 2. Your goal is to begin the discussion of whether you have all of the talent you need allocated among all of the different perspectives and personalities that you want. Do you have too many tech leaders? Too many visionaries? Not enough people with the patience to balance the checkbook? What do you see in the mix of logos and pathos? Every strong leadership team has a place at the table for those who lead with their heads and those who lead with their hearts. Don't underestimate the value of either group.

After the Pizza Party, you may decide that your group is too large or too small or that it is just the wrong mix. In that case, try again until you find the right mix. Do not go past this chapter and the exercises in it until you are certain that the Founders' Table is filled with the right leadership team. After the meeting, hand out the next few Pizza Party prep exercises and set the next Pizza Party date.

Lesson 2: Get to Know the Founders Really Well

Building a strong team takes time and trust. It requires members to be honest with themselves and one another. The saying that your chain is only as strong as its weakest link is true. Each founder is a link in the chain. Each founder has vulnerabilities, weaknesses, real and imagined limitations …

Founders are also a part of families. They are breadwinners and parents and adult caregivers. Their responsibilities outside of the company are not necessarily weaknesses, but honesty about personal needs is critical to strengthening the whole group.

Economic demands are also critical. Three founders of similar age, income, and educational background may have very different economic needs and goals. Risk tolerance is a factor. Student or consumer debt is a factor. Obligations to provide financial support to others is a factor.

A strong leadership team understands the weaknesses in the chain and plans for ways to strengthen the bonds.

A weak leadership team bulldozes forward, assuming that everyone is on the same page with the same goals, timelines, and economic expectations.

I have been a part of both types of teams. Sometimes the weakness of the links cannot be overcome in later stages without buying out the founder whose link has failed. This can be a big mess. Avoid it with honest and open communication up front.

Diamond Productions Story. The founders of Diamond Productions thought they knew one another well. They had worked together on various projects over the years and assumed they would have no trouble building a highly functional team. As they shared their personal struggles, stories, and goals in Pizza Party 2, they learned that Christine was really burned out with her work and considering taking a few years to live abroad and work remotely to clear her head and hit reset. She was still very interested in launching Diamond Productions but felt that she would contribute better if she could put some distance physically and emotionally between her past and present. This was news to the others. They had envisioned launching a vibrant, in-person office culture in a location that would inspire both the founders and the next generation of minority and women producers, writers, and directors. Remote participation by one of the members required some rethinking. As they continued to work through the Pizza Party homework and the rest of this book, they reimagined their business plan in a more flexible, virtual environment, not tied to a specific physical location but rather to a series of in-person meetups and special events.

Camp Car Story. Alicia and Michelle had worked together for years sharing the joys and challenges of raising kids and juggling their jobs. They thought they knew each other well and assumed they could skip the lesson 2 work. But they did it anyway. One of the  things they learned was that Alicia's parents were becoming more and more dependent on her and her sister emotionally, logistically, and for financial management. This was draining Alicia's enthusiasm for taking on new ventures. Her father would likely enter hospice that summer, and her mother could not manage the finances or an independent household. Alicia had adequate support from her husband and sister. But she needed Michelle to know that the timelines might have to be fluid for their business launch to accommodate the unpredictable demands of caregiving. Michelle was glad Alicia was honest about this. It made it easier for both of them to validate and support each other in leadership. And it encouraged both of them to do some cross-training around each other's strengths and skill sets. In the end, they shared responsibilities and overlapped duties more than they might have otherwise done, so that both of them could take time off for personal reasons without tanking the business.

Pizza Party 2—Let's Get Personal and Choose Some Hats

Schedule another ninety-minute Pizza Party and assign everyone Pizza Party 2 prep exercises. Founders will come to the Pizza Party having reflected on their personal objectives and limitations.

Note that some may balk at this homework. Encourage them individually by emphasizing the importance of building a team.

Make time in this Pizza Party for each person to share their answers to the prep exercises. You can either have each go all of the way through the survey, or you can take turns answering questions by category. Some teams may find it helpful to share the answers in advance. Respect the confidentiality of your Founders' Table.

Prep Exercise 1 focuses on the individual's life and goals outside the company. Prep Exercise 2 encourages reflection on an individual's contributions inside the company. Prep Exercise 3 helps the team identify specific roles required in leadership. Prep Exercise 4 synthesizes the goals and roles into an integrated roster and to evaluate what might be missing or duplicated in your starting lineup.

If someone says, "It doesn't matter what my spouse thinks," they are either on the brink of divorce or are completely myopic about the impact of personal relationships and commitments on the risk taking and sacrifices required to sit at the Founders' Table.

Many of the choices the company makes will impact the personal financial lives of the founders, including choice of entity, tax elections, buy-sell agreements, and exit strategies. These decisions literally hit home. Open up. Talk about your families and goals. It will help you make intelligent choices later.

Respect the confidentiality of your Founders' Table. If someone asks or has concerns about confidentiality, it may be appropriate to sign a mutual nondisclosure agreement at this point in time.

After discussing Prep Exercises 1 and 2, work together to complete Prep Exercises 3 and 4. You may need a second Pizza Party for this work if you are in the early stages of developing your business plan and don't know what resources you may need.

Lesson 3: How Many Hats and Who Wears Them?

When counseling clients, I often bring a collection of hats to the conference room (or draw them badly on the whiteboard). Baseball hats for officers with daily operations responsibility. Sombreros for investors (resting in the shade, waiting for their money). Captain's hats for active, strong leaders. Ski caps for founders … Sometimes a single person in the room will end up wearing four or five hats at once.

The hat exercise can also be useful in defining specific leadership roles: a ball cap for the finance genius; a beret for the creative leader; a fancy, attention-grabbing hat for the marketing guru; a collection of helmets for the visionaries who never seem to get concussions or doubts as quickly as others.

It is obvious that you cannot successfully launch a company with six visionaries who have no finance or technical skills. You cannot successfully launch a company with three techies and no visionaries. You cannot successfully launch a company without marketing, operational leadership, compliance, and someone in a trusted, senior leadership role who has strong interpersonal skills and is willing to be a peacemaker.

In the remaining prep exercises for Pizza Party 2, figure out who is wearing which hats. You may have more hats than talent in some areas and more talent than hats in others. These exercises will help you focus on where you need to fill the gaps and possibly encourage growth into roles.

Prep Exercises 3 and 4 are *do-annually* homework. In an annual leadership retreat, reflect on the fit and function of each member of the leadership team. Also revisit the answers given in Prep Exercises 1 and 2 from this lesson. It may be appropriate to bring in a leadership or team-building coach to facilitate honest discussion as your company and your team evolves.

Lesson 4: Identify Your Leadership Paradigm

Now that you've identified the founders and their respective roles or hats, you need to identify which leadership paradigm fits your group. Do you have several people wearing captain's hats or just one? Do you have a group that prefers (and maybe requires) consensus building, or do most founders defer to one or two strong leaders?

Refer to the descriptions below and choose what seems to suit the existing dynamic of the group most. Keep in mind that this will likely change over time—and it should change over time. But it is valuable to choose a model to start your journey and create governance rules consistent with the founders' expectations in the context of that model.

Some groups will find this exercise easy. More than half of my start-up clients are naturally enlightened dictatorships. A single, strong leader owns the idea, drives the process, brings the resources (including some capital), and is the force of nature making it all happen. Another quarter of my clients are determined to launch as fifty/fifty ventures. Then the remaining quarter are a mixed bag of mature companies with more representative structures or oligarchies.

Some factors to consider:

- personalities
- entitlement based on original idea
- skill sets
- outside commitments or limitations
- money
- tiers of leadership
- individual goals and timelines

Review the models below and decide which fits your vision right now, in twelve months, and in twenty-four months.

Enlightened dictatorship. This is most common when there is a strong personality at the helm who has come up with *the great idea*, done some of the funding, assembled the team, and been the primary driving force to this point. The author of a book is its enlightened dictator. What other examples come to mind? This can be a very stable and successful initial leadership model if all founders and others consent to it and if the boundaries are clearly stated from the outset. Some companies exist as enlightened dictatorships all the way to an exit or to a generational change.

Oligarchy—a small group of equal leaders. This model is less stable over the long term than an enlightened dictatorship simply because it depends on a small group (three to five people at most) aligning their interests, energy, economics, and passions for an extended period of time. Service companies such as accounting firms, doctors' offices, law firms, architects, and so on often start as oligarchies. So do younger founders who are launching businesses at a period in their lives when all members of the group have discretionary time and energy to commit to the new deal. To make this work, the oligarchy will need to build a great deal of trust and will need to focus carefully on the Decision Matrix in the next chapter.

Democracy. This is the default model if there is not a single strong leader and there are more people in the founders' group than can reasonably function as an oligarchy. It is rarely stable for companies or countries over long periods of stressful and unpredictable growth. Service companies often start this way but slip quickly but informally into dictatorships or oligarchies without thinking through minority protection rights.

Representative democracy. This is the classic corporate model and is most common and most stable for mature enterprises with fiscal and directional stability. A corporation consists of shareholders/investors who are generally passive, reserving the right to vote by selling their interests or by electing directors. The directors represent the investor/money interest and provide big-picture and directional guidance (hence the word *director*). Directors, in turn, elect officers to run the day-to-day business. It is rare for this model to work in classic corporate form for start-up or evolving companies. But variations on the theme are endless—and a good lawyer can help you work through how to balance interests and talents in this format.

Fifty/fifty. *Warning*: this is the least stable and most dangerous leadership model. Two, four, or even six individuals rarely see eye to eye for extended periods through growth, stress, change, and evolution in the business and personal lives. Deadlock is common and very difficult. There are some short-term ways to create a bridge between the fifty/fifty structure and a more stable model. But always beware that the devil of deadlock looms in the background. Some appropriate uses of this model include well-thought-out joint ventures that can easily separate if there are differences of opinion or priorities and ventures led by very mature and seasoned leaders with advisory boards.

Camp Car Story. Alicia and Michelle decide that they are comfortable with the fragile fifty/fifty leadership structure even after heeding the warnings. But they spend time and energy clearly delineating the lines of authority that each hold. They follow the basic rule that they will defer the last vote to the person who is either most experienced or most passionate about an issue. And they worked hard with their outside adviser, Charlie, to create a comprehensive Decision Matrix.

Law Firm Story. Our law firm founders decided on a modified representative democracy model where each would take turns being the president in two-year shifts, beginning with Shayla. They defined the responsibilities of the president clearly in the Decision Matrix. They reserved some major decisions for unanimous consent, including adding a new partner, committing to long-term or expensive contracts or loans, and taking on high-risk cases. And they created another category of important strategic decisions requiring two of the three (majority)

approval, including renewing the lease, committing to IT and data security systems, and hiring shared staff.

Rocket Fuel and Diamond Productions Stories: Both Rocket Fuel and Diamond Productions start out as oligarchies (or small democracies). They do assign some responsibilities to particular founders in the Decision Matrix. But they also are counting on rule by consensus for the first eighteen months as they develop their vision more completely. They don't take the Decision Matrix exercise very seriously at first. Rocket Fuel has a leadership breakdown in the eighth month on the eve of launching their first round of a capital raise. It is taking too much time to build consensus around every little thing. They revisit lesson 2 and lesson 3 at a new Pizza Party. Sally has taken a solid and decisive hand at the helm, even when not asked or clearly authorized to do so. They elect her president and give her strong authority over operations and funding. The other two founders also take on specialized leadership roles.

Pizza Party 3—Leadership Paradigm and Decision Matrix

By now you have settled on a core group of founders and identified each other's strengths and weaknesses. At this Pizza Party, start by guessing your leadership paradigm, then test your guess with the following series of role-playing exercises. Consider each business puzzle a few times, discuss your respective opinions and proposals, then see if your chosen leadership paradigm holds up to reaching an actual decision for the company.

Practice Problem 1: Hiring an Accounting Firm or Law Firm

One of the first decisions you will make is building your team of trusted outside advisers. How will you choose? What process will you follow to develop a strong list of candidate advisers, interviewing them, developing a project list and a budget, and ultimately signing an engagement letter?

Practice Problem 2: Signing a Lease

Perhaps after your COVID quarantine, you won't need to identify a physical space for your new company's home. But assume you do. What factors should you consider in selecting a space? What budget do you have for leasing space? What are the top three factors you need to consider other than price? Do you need an exclusive space, or will share-space facilities work for you? Are you willing to sign a personal guarantee to back the lease? How will you go about reviewing and negotiating the lease and arranging for a move/occupancy? Who plays key roles in searching for property, reviewing contracts, figuring out the finances, scheduling the move, and so on?

Practice Problem 3: Courting an Angel Investor

Later in this book, we address the different types of investors. Assume for now that there are two wealthy and entrepreneurial angel investors who have met one or more of your founders at a local meetup. Who is going to approach these prospective investors? How will you prepare for a meeting? What resources do you need to develop for a potential meeting? Who has the last say over any written materials?

Practice Problem 4: Making a Press Release

Sometime soon after launch, you will want to announce your company to the world as part of a B to B or B to C rollout (that is "business to business" or "business to consumer"). Draft a sample press release based on the vision you have today. Who oversees developing the strategy? Who drafts the release? Who handles the press and other inquiries that may arise after the release is made?

Lesson 5: Complete Your Decision Matrix

Finding the right roles is sometimes a trial-and-error process. Most companies start out with some assumptions about the talents and interests of each of the founders. After some months (or years). they modify those assumptions based on real-life experiences. Almost always, founders grow in their skills and interests as they are challenged by new tasks outside of their comfort zones.

Your founders are ahead of the curve if you've worked carefully through the Human Factors, clarified your roles, and identified your leadership paradigm.

What is a Decision Matrix? It is simply a chore chart. A clear statement of assigned roles from the macro to the micro. It helps your team focus in advance of controversies on decisions around running out of funds, borrowing money, hiring and firing, developing budgets, managing client relationships, creative vision, compliance with laws, and other tasks large and small. It helps you imagine the future in the context of navigating problems with a team. For the Decision Matrix to be meaningful, both the list of decisions and the matrix of decision-makers must be complete.

Look at the examples and read the stories before trying to build your own Decision Matrix.

Prior to the next Pizza Party, assign one of the founders the homework of adapting one of the Decision Matrix forms found in the appendix to the specific circumstances and business operations of your company. Review all the forms even if you have already chosen your leadership paradigm. Refer back to the Prep Exercises 2 and 3 from Pizza Party 2 to see how the roles fit together. The founder who draws the straw on homework should review all the Decision Matrix examples and come up with a rough draft using the following guidelines:

1. Review the laundry list of decisions in the first column and modify as necessary.
2. Look over the top row of decision-makers. This row varies based on the leadership paradigms.
3. Mix and match. You may start with the decisions from the real estate example and add it to the fifty/fifty leadership paradigm

4. Adapt the grids to your team. Change the column titles. For example, with a 50/50 venture, you may have four columns: Founder 1, Founder 2, Both, and Advisory Board. For an Enlighted Dictator venture, you may have three columns: Enlightened Dictator, a majority, and unanimous consent. The variations are endless and should reflect how you intend to make decisions and hold each other accountable.

5. Circulate the modified form to each founder and ask them to fill in the blanks by checking columns on who votes prior to the meeting. Each founder should take a shot at assigning the decisions to the parties listed in the columns. Column 1 is the most important decision-maker and should be making most of the decisions. The other columns set out decisions that require special approval by defined parties in interest—like a supermajority—or that can be safely and regularly delegated to officers.

6. While munching on pizza slices (NY or Chicago style?), compare your answers and reconcile the differences in the matrix.

When you are customizing your Decision Matrix, consider the following examples:

Real Estate: If you are investing in real estate, you may need to add specific decisions related to selection of properties, financing, refinancing, like-kind exchanges, borrowing for capital improvements, tenant issues, taxes, and raising capital. Both operating and capital budget development and approval are important.

Software Companies: If you are developing IP, you may need to add specific engineering and project milestone decisions. You will also need capital raising, budget, and marketing plans.

Services Companies: If you are launching a services company (accounting, law, architecture, consulting, etc.) you may want client-specific decisions or personnel-specific decisions.

Construction Companies: Depending on the size of the company, roles may divide naturally among project management, customer relations, and accounting activities. With a small company, an enlightened dictator may wear all of these hats daily. In a larger company, roles will be divided, and a more traditional shareholder/board/officer structure may make sense.

The Decision Matrix process is *do-annually* assignment. Roles change. Leadership paradigms change. People change.

Consider going back for your annual checkup with your attorney with an updated Decision Matrix to attach to your limited liability company agreement or your shareholders' agreement.

Consider updating it at major milestones to reflect your new leadership paradigm and additional roles and decisions.

Rocket Fuel Story. Rocket Fuel's leadership team dynamics evolved rapidly over the first eighteen months of operations, growth, fund-raising, and expansion. They had sufficient funding to dive deep into the technology and manufacturing side of the business. Someone needed to oversee that effort and own the decisions. Paired with the technology development was legal protection through trademarks,  patents, copyrights, and other intellectual property protections discussed later in this book. Sally took on the day-to-day operational leadership of the company. But after the six-month review of the Decision Matrix, the founders decided that Luke needed to step up and be given both the authority and responsibility for the basket of tasks around technology and legal protection. By the end of their second year, they had added an employee to head up the sales channels and had delegated responsibilities to her. With growth came complexity and specialization. The original groupthink model that worked for graduate students completing joint research projects was not effective for rapid and efficient commercial operations.

Conclusion

Now that you've got your team together, you're ready to start tackling other issues. Figuring out the Human Factor is an essential first step from idea to enterprise that cannot be skipped over. The first thirty days of starting your business should be centered in working through the founders and identifying key leadership roles. You will be better equipped to solve the hard problems later on if you have established a strong core group with open communication and trust. Scribbling who does what and who knows what haphazardly on the back of a napkin won't cut it. You need to put time and energy into this. The following chapters in this book will guide you through everything from choice of entity to trademarks. But don't forget your pizza parties; come back to these lessons and their respective homework annually with your team. Once you have established a core group of founders, asked the tough questions around the Human Factors and roles, and sorted out your Decision Matrix, you're ready to take the next step from idea to enterprise by raising some money.

CHAPTER 2

Cap Tables, Endgame Goals, and People with Money to Invest

Sort Out Your Cap Table

A" Cap Table" is a summary of ownership that shows percentage ownership, perhaps the number of units or shares, the class of equity, and, in an LLC, the initial capital contribution of each person. This Cap Table changes each time a new investor is added, or an existing investor sells its interest. Adding new classes (for series A or other classes) requires restating the Cap Table.

This chapter assumes you have formed an LLC (see later chapter for advice on choice of entity). If you have formed a corporation, you will maintain a stock registry as the official legal document showing ownership, shares, and certificate numbers. Most corporations *also* keep a Cap Table as part of their accounting records.

In the examples below, the LLC awards "units" to the founders. Units are the equivalent of shares in a corporation. Corporations are required to issue shares and to document the shares with certificates. LLCs and partnerships are not required to issue units and can (and often do) record ownership in percentages throughout their lives if they have few changes in ownership. LLCs and partnerships do not have to issue certificates, and it is often a record-keeping headache to try to maintain certificate records in private companies.

Your first Cap Table will focus on founders and their ownership interests. If you plan to raise capital, then the Cap Table will change as new money comes in the door. Note that the first new money almost always comes in as "common equity" or "common shares," with the same basic voting and economic rights as founders who contribute money.

In Chapter 1, you figured out who is at the table, why, and what their roles are. But you have not yet decided how to allocate ownership percentages/shares among the founders. This can be a tricky task if there are players with very different roles and contributions. It is fundamentally a negotiation exercise.

Note that in the examples below, the capital contributions do not match the percentage ownership. In LLCs taxed as partnerships, this is common, and those putting in money will get their funds out first. In corporations, the disparity is permanent. There are ways to compensate key people who are not founders with equity. But in this chapter, we are just discussing equity for founders and early-stage investors.

If your company has five founders and the leadership paradigm is an enlightened dictatorship, it is likely that the primary leader has a larger ownership percentage than the others. The company's initial Cap Table reflects the ownership differences, the differences in cash and in-kind value contributed, and basic data (addresses, tax identification numbers, etc.) that an accountant might need to know for preparing tax returns.

Cap Table

January 1, 2022
NEWCO, LLC

Name, Address, FEIN	Sharing Ratio	Initial Capital Contribution
Supreme leader	75%	$25,000
Creative guru	15%	$25,000 (in-kind value)
Finance wonk	5%	$1,500
Trusted mentor	2.5%	$10,000
Marketing guru with people skills	2.5%	$0
	100.00%	**$61,500**

In the next example, there are two owners who make equal contributions and have equal rights in profits and votes.

Cap Table

January 1, 2022
NEWCO, LLC

Name, Address, FEIN	Sharing Ratio	Units	Initial Capital Contribution
Alicia	50%	5,000	$5,000
Michelle	50%	5,000	$5,000
	100%	10,000	$10,000

It is necessary to sort out your Cap Table before moving to the next step of raising money.

If you *are* raising money, you may want to create a pro forma Cap Table to make hypothetical space in your Cap Table for future equity awards (restricted stock, restricted units, options, etc.). Many companies reserve between 15 percent and 25 percent of their founders' equity to award to parties who did not make it to the Founders' Table but who will have value to contribute in the future.

In the example below, the company with five founders assumes that they should reserve 20 percent of ownership for issuance to other Key Contributors. So, they prepare a pro forma Cap Table to share with investors. That way, investors see the plan for growth. This is just one of many ways to allocate ownership for present and future contributors.

Pro Forma Cap Table

January 1, 2022
NEWCO, LLC

Name, Address, FEIN	Sharing Ratio	Initial Capital Contribution
Key leader	60%	$25,000
Creative guru	12%	$25,000 (in-kind value)
Finance wonk	4%	$1,500
Trusted mentor	2%	$10,000
Marketing guru with people skills	2%	$0
Reserved for future Key Contributors	20%	
	100%	**$61,500**

There are endless variations on these themes. The original Cap Table for a company that intends to reward Key Contributors and raise money will change often. Your accountant will use this as a starting document to create tax reporting. When you start making money, the Cap Table will be a guiding document on how to distribute the profits. If you lose money in the start-up phase, it may be a guide on how losses are allocated. Keep it updated and make sure a signed official version is always in your corporate records.

Raising Money: Begin with the End in Mind and Define Your Goals

Before you raise any money, you need to ask yourself some questions. Are you building a two-location gourmet bakery in your hometown, or are you looking to sell your company for $30mm in five years to a private equity group? Two extreme examples, yes, but it is important to know where you are going before you start raising money. One path is *build and hold*, and the other is a *sell out soon* path. Both paths are legitimate, but they are extremely different. The choice of path influences valuation, who is a likely investor, and the type of investment you can reasonably undertake. Chapter 3 addresses goal setting in more detail. For now, keep your endgame in mind as you explore funding options.

A mom-and-pop bakery may be creating a legacy for generations in their community. They will look for money from locals who want the best eclairs and croissants just around the corner.

On the other hand, a nationwide chain of fast and casual cafes is looking to build a global brand instead of a local reputation for the best croissants on the block.

Initially, the funding for most businesses comes either from the founders or from the Fs: friends, family, and fools.

The trickiest issue around raising money is *valuation*. There is no single right answer. And lawyers can't really help you with this.

In the earliest stages, you can avoid the issue by raising money through convertible notes, or just charging everything to your credit card or drawing on your savings. Your FFFs (see below) will likely lend you some money to get you started without having a valuation. But this won't last forever.

Eventually, you'll need to figure out what you think your company is worth and what others think it is worth. That is a big milestone in the path from idea to enterprise and will require more than thoughts scribbled on the back of a napkin. When you are ready to take that leap, you start raising money by selling pieces of the pie—the equity—to outsiders and by exchanging those initial notes for equity.

Below you will find a sample path to help you navigate raising money for your company. Note that there are excellent books dedicated just to this topic. The information in this chapter is a beginning guide. Find a mentor in an angel network to help guide you further. This book does not address the securities laws that govern all issuances of equity and debt out of a private company. Anytime you sell equity, take money through notes, or raise capital of any kind, hire an experienced securities lawyer to help you navigate the path, give adequate disclosures, and comply with the law.

FFF: Friends, Fools, and Family. In the earliest stages of your company, you will need money but will really have nothing to show other than your personal good character, enthusiasm, and great ideas. While good ideas written on the back of napkins or hastily summarized in text messages seem to have been sufficient for certain dot-com boom companies, they likely won't be enough for you to attract the attention of a buyer or a giant investor. The Fs are the cheerleaders. They are investing in the founders—and the reputation and goodwill of the founders. Their rights as investors are defined in the company agreement (or operating agreement) for LLCs and in the certificate of formation for corporations.

Let's think back to the beginning of this chapter and what kind of company you are building. A mom-and-pop bakery in your hometown will most likely seek investments from locals. By contrast, a nationwide chain will likely start with the Fs but then move on to angels and crowdfunding.

> **Key Information:** Any offering of equity from a private company is a private offering. All private offerings (of equity or debt) are subject to complicated securities laws at the federal and state level. If done properly, the private offerings can be exempt offerings under the securities laws, and the issuers will have certain protections against investors who later come back and sue the issuers. If not done properly, a private offering can create personal liability exposure for the officers, directors, and others leading the offering. Do not try to raise money without legal advice.

This seed funding can include *angels* who are normally *accredited investors* (securities law term that your lawyer will explain) who make relatively small strategic investments alongside founders and their Fs because they believe in the business and the founders. They don't expect any special returns or special treatment. However, angels are often really useful, smart, experienced people who should be on your board or act as a strategic adviser. If that's the case, buy them a beer, some pizza, and a copy of this book when they invest in you—and listen to them.

> **Camp Car Story.** Our characters Alicia and Michelle have realized their end goal. After building their alternative car rental business, they plan to search for a buyer, ideally joining a chain. With this goal in mind, Alicia and Michelle can start raising money. Now, this is a bootstrap operation. In the beginning, they will need to rely on their FFFs to finance vehicle purchases, employees, RV park concessions,

and so on. With a smart and solid business plan, they hope to attract some angel investors as well. Alicia's contact at a major car manufacturer may be helpful here if they can find an angel investor with industry knowledge.

Angels. When you exhaust the friends, fools, and family (and likely your credit cards too), you'll want to expand your network to include some nice, supportive rich people. An ideal angel investor is helpful, courteous, patient, kind, and well connected. If this sounds like a grown-up Boy Scout or Girl Scout, it should. You want angels who are good mentors with some industry knowledge and real-life experience. You may also want angels who believe totally in you, are emotionally supportive, and are very patient about your need to make mistakes. In return, angels want you to be honest about your plans and your mistakes, communicate frequently, and work hard. Angels may ask for a larger percentage of the company than the FFFs, but they will come in as common equity without a preferred return and without special voting rights.

Using the example above, the revised Cap Table below shows an angel investment of $100,000 in exchange for 10 percent of the company. Valuation is discussed below in more detail. But this investment indicates that the example company has a valuation of $1,000,000.

You will note that we've added "units" to this table. A company adding investors will at some point begin issuing certificates and denominating ownership in units. Of course, a corporation has to do this from the beginning. Cap tables become more confusing as more details are added over time, so owners sometimes defer adding the complexity of units until they have moved into later rounds of equity.

You will also note that this "angel round" dilutes not only the existing founders but also the percentage available for future noncash contributors. This is not always the case. This is only one way to organize your equity; there are hundreds of variations on the theme that can be negotiated among the founders, angels, and future investors.

Your lawyer and investment banker (when you grow large enough to need one) will advise you on what is normal in your industry for Cap Table organization as well as what may be most effective in attracting both funds and talent.

Pro Forma Cap Table after Angel Investment

January 1, 2022
NEWCO, LLC

Name, Address, FEIN	Sharing Ratio	Units	Initial Capital Contribution
Key leader	54%	5,400	$25,000
Creative guru	10.8%	1,080	$25,000 (in-kind value)
Finance wonk	3.6%	360	$1,500
Trusted mentor	1.8%	180	$10,000
Marketing genius with people skills	1.8%	180	$0
Angel investor	10%	1,000	$100,000
Reserved for future Key Contributors	18%	1,800	
	100%	**10,720**	**$161,500**

Pantheon of Women Story. I launched a film production company with a group of enthusiastic and creative women who saw film as a way to change the way the world perceives women. We adopted the slogan "If you can see it, you can be it" and struck out to make films that would "Entertain, Educate, and Inspire." This was a lot of scribbles on a napkin without any proof of revenue. Our angel investors provided funding for our first film purely out of faith that we would do our best to make a great movie and get it out to the world. They followed up with three more investments that ultimately did not result in finished films. At each step, we leaned on them for input and energy as well as funds. With one project that was at a very early stage, we took funds in the form of convertible notes because we just were not sure exactly where the deal was headed but had to show the writers, we had funds on deposit. We repaid those notes. On each project, we were honest about the changes in direction, and we gave them the remaining unspent funds back. Ultimately, we made one and a half films and started two others. It was very, very hard to meet with our supportive angels to give them back the unspent funds. But almost all of them were encouraging and supportive to the very end. Several said they would invest again—and one even wanted me to keep her money in escrow for my next project. These were true angels who believed in me even when I failed to complete the projects we planned.

Crowdfunding or Kickstarter Campaigns. A possible next tier of funding (or source pursued in parallel with FFFs and angels) works for many consumer-facing businesses and retail products.

There are legal considerations to doing a crowdfunded equity offering. Websites and platforms designed to launch, manage, or facilitate crowdfunding may or may not provide the necessary legal advice and framework to clearly set out the rights of these investors. No one ever gives you money without expecting to get something back. It is important to remember the difference between a donation or gift and an investment.

Investments create equity ownership and rights as owners in the company. Their rights as investors must be defined in the amended legal documents.

Gifts and donations (sometimes in the form of subscriptions or prepayments for merch) do not create equity interests. If you are giving away tickets or T-shirts or lunch with the founder, you are likely not conducting a securities offering.

Crowdfunding became very popular after the 2008 Recession in part because Congress created some special exceptions to the securities laws to make it easier and in part because so many people lost money on Wall Street that they decided to make small bets on Main Street. This was also the beginning of really sophisticated social media campaigns and targeted advertising through Facebook and other platforms.

Even nonprofits and political campaigns joined in by moving their fundraising online. Anytime you see a contest or a "free" giveaway, you're seeing a version of crowdfunding.

A recent consumer success story is Nuubii—creators of an innovative women's bra. They used their broad list of connections to create a targeted mailing list of interested parties and encouraged each to put in some money (a few hundred dollars) and receive a couple of bras in the mail. When they received enough seed capital, they started making and sending out bras. That *kickstarted* their sales, created a customer list, and provided seed capital all in one exercise. It took a lot of work and about six months … but it worked.

Series A. This is where the real money comes in and where the lawyers and possibly investment bankers get involved. Series A (in an LLC, often class C) investors want rights in exchange for their larger cash outlay. Their rights are usually negotiated in a *term sheet*. They do diligence on the company and expect to become informed of both your track record and your business plans through an *offering memorandum* or something similar. They *subscribe* to purchase equity through a *subscription agreement* and become owners when they put their cash into the company. This is a complex legal project requiring lawyers with securities, tax, intellectual property, and sometimes other kinds of expertise. Expect to spend between 3 percent and 5 percent of the amount of your capital raised on legal fees. At this level, your investors (including your angels) will want you to have clear answers about tough and complicated legal topics like these:

- antidilution
- right of first refusal (ROFR) in future rounds
- board seats
- preferred return of capital
- other minority and money protections
- series B, C, and D (in an LLC, classes D, E, and F)—effectively larger versions of series A; demanding more rights at each round

This will be your first really big negotiation exercise.

Rocket Fuel Story. The founders were really lucky to skip the FFF stage by winning the Rice Business Competition. That seed capital got them enough traction to easily raise more money from angels in the Houston community of technology and space industry investors. Like many new industrial product companies, there is a long ramp up for this company. They raise their series A funding of $5 million with a single lead investor putting in $2.5 million. At the time of the raise, the investors and founders negotiated a company valuation of $25 million, so the series A represented a 20 percent interest.

Bridge Notes / Convertible Notes. Sometimes it is just impossible to get consensus around valuation (see below), and yet there are investors willing to bet on you and your idea before it is an enterprise. A neat legal trick is to borrow money from those committed and friendly angels while giving them the right to convert their notes into equity at a later date. How does this work? Generally, the prospective investor offers to loan you funds for a relatively short (six to twenty-four months) period of time to use as working capital while you simultaneously lay the groundwork for a round of equity funding. Interest rates on these loans are often high (reflecting the risk), but both the principal and the interest can be converted into new equity when you sell to another investor or group of investors. It is common, though not always necessary, to offer the friendly lender a bonus for being a first mover in the form of a discount on the price of the equity to be purchased with the converted note value. This is a very common tool—but get the lawyers involved. You are issuing real debt, and the whole project is governed by securities laws as well as lending laws and more. It is not for amateurs who find forms on the internet.

> Mariella has a great idea for her second company. She's built a great business with her brother and now wants to launch Company II. This time, she borrows $500,000 from a couple of customers who see the value of Company II. After she launches and meets a couple of milestones, the customers agree (this time as angels) to convert their loans into equity and to put in $2mm more. Mariella brings the angels in as co-owners and now hopes to grow her company without additional investments by reinvesting the profits into growth.

SBA Loans and Bank Loans. Banks generally are wary of lending funds to true start-up companies. If you have a large personal line of credit, your bank may let you draw that down to fund part of the venture. But that loan likely won't get you very far, and it puts your personal credit at risk. The Small Business Association partners with financial institutions (including banks and credit unions and community banks) to make funds available on special terms to small businesses. Applying for an SBA loan can be like applying for student financial aid or a home mortgage. The process is cumbersome and requires disclosure of significant personal details about the founders' finances. SBA loans almost always require personal guarantees and sometimes require founders to pledge personal assets as collateral. If your endgame is build and hold, then viewing the SBA loan as an equivalent to a home mortgage may make sense. If you plan to sell out soon and/or will need substantial capital from additional investors, you may want to skip this step.

Valuation. Remember that valuing the company is part of all fundraising. Lawyers *are not* qualified to tell you what your company is worth. Neither is your mom. In many situations, it is a best guess undertaking that gets negotiated along the way with prospective investors. If you value your company too high, you may drive away investors. If you value it too low, you are likely to give away too much. If this is confusing, watch a few episodes of *Shark Tank*, and you'll get the idea of the negotiation of value process. Mr. Wonderful is wonderfully blunt about sharing his opinions with companies that value themselves aggressively. (Note that the sharks are angel investors … and they structure most of their investments as common equity).

For those not headed to *Shark Tank*, there are two ways to approach valuation before you negotiate with investors—the sales guy approach and the numbers guy approach. Neither is necessarily right or wrong. And the insights of both approaches are valuable. Ultimately, your company is worth what an investor will say it is worth when the investor puts in the cash, but you have to start somewhere:

Sales Guy Approach. Picks a number out of the air and sells the idea to all investors successfully.

Benefit: easy.

Cost: may bite you later in a down round if the value was set too high initially.

Numbers Guy Approach. Does a bunch of research on comparable companies, documents it, prepares detailed projections, then pulls a number out of the sky and has to sell it.

Benefit: looks like it is founded in empirical data and can be supported.

Cost: the data is suspect because you are doing something inherently novel.

Every team of founders will have—or should have—both a sales guy and a numbers guy.

They will always be in conflict—and that is a good thing. Investors may have a strong opinion about your proposed valuation, as you probably know from watching episodes of *Shark Tank*.

The lawyer should not and ethically cannot be your tiebreaker.

Special note: Appraisals are fairly suspect for early-stage companies. They many times are not worth the money as a substitute for the work of your own numbers guy. You will get to know the appraisers later in the exit process, for succession planning and sometimes for gifting. But it may not be helpful to bring them in at this early stage.

Don't forget: Before you start raising money, you must try to envision the future of your company. The small, local bakery or the global chain establishment? Both are valuable and legitimate, but the distinction is important. Next chapter, you will start focusing on those goals.

CHAPTER 3

Goals

If you are reading this book, you are already pretty good at setting macro goals and micro goals and may have already achieved some of the first micro goals for your company.

What does this have to do with your lawyer? Well, your lawyer's services cost money. Setting your priorities for the business will help you set your priorities with your lawyer. They will also guide your lawyer in selecting the right level of detail or complexity for your particular legal projects. Communicate your goals clearly to your advisers so they can align their work to your budget, your priorities, and your timeline.

Create a ninety-day timeline as you go through this chapter. And remember that the first thirty days or so should be dedicated to sorting out the people. Tackling the lessons in chapter 1 should always be your first goal, and the rest will follow. Raising capital, protecting your IP, and hiring a team of experts will fall along the path somewhere too. These are micro goals. After setting the macro goal, start filling in the blanks on the timeline with micro goals.

What Is Your Macro Goal?

You have two choices when it comes to your macro goal. They are:

- sell out soon versus build and hold
- exit gains versus recurring income

Sell Out Soon

This is the business model of the dot-com boom. It is the business goal of house flippers. It is the business goal of Girl Scouts selling cookies and Boy Scouts selling Christmas greenery. Put together the fundamentals of the business in a way that demonstrates proof of concept to a target audience. Then court a suitor and sell out for a profit as quickly as reasonable.

Your short and midterm goals need not relate to maximizing cash flow or making expensive long-term investments.

Build and Hold

If you want recurring income, you are probably in the build and hold category. You need to tell that to your investors, your employees, your spouse, your cofounders, and everyone else. Managing for positive cash flow will be important as a short- or medium-term goal. Strategically planning capital investments with the goal of lowering the cost of financing those investments may be very important.

What Are Micro Goals?

Once you have identified your macro goal, you need to identify five to seven intermediate goals to accomplish over a finite (and short) period (such as a fiscal quarter).

> **Rocket Fuel Story.** Luke, Marco, and Sally's macro goal is to sell out soon. They need to establish short- and medium-term micro goals that will help them prove three principal things to a potential buyer:

1. Their Rocket Fuel product works as promised.
2. There is a market for the Rocket Fuel at a price point that results in realistic margins.
3. They own all the IP and technology required to manufacture and sell the Rocket Fuel.

> With those requirements in mind, they might set out some midterm micro goals that include doing the following:

1. Research and invest in patenting their technology.
2. Attract and retain top talent on the research and development side.
3. Begin relationships with future purchasers, such as SpaceX, perhaps by seeking the future purchasers as co-investors.

> On a do-next-week level of micro goals, they might need to hire an IP lawyer who can go head-to-head with the Rice University IP team to clarify the joint ownership of any IP developments. They might join the Houston entrepreneurial communities that have developed around space technology to build a network of outside advisers (and possible investors) who can make introductions into the right purchasers.

> Other important micro goals that should happen in parallel path include identifying the founding team, finding a cofounder/partner providing resources related to intellectual property rights, and establishing a robust business plan to attract investors. Once completed, they can move on to more goals, such as beginning design on their Rocket Fuel product, reviewing regulations, and raising capital.

> **Diamond Productions Story.** Christine, Elara, and Tomas's macro goal is to build and hold. They will need to establish short- and medium-term micro goals that will attract filmmakers to Diamond Productions so that they can start raising capital.

Micro goals for the first quarter are:

- Identify the founding leadership team.
- Set a seed capital budget and raise seed funds.

Micro goals for the second quarter are:

- Identify first film and create production team.
- Develop a plan to raise capital.

Micro goals for the third quarter are:

- Get the legal and financial house in order.
- Work through team-building issues (see Chapter 1).
- Develop project plan for film 1.

Camp Car Story. Alicia and Michelle's macro goal is to sell out soon. Their micro goals will reflect the need to attract potential buyers, such as Zip Car. Some of their midterm micro goals include:

1. Find major car manufacturer to partner with for their fleet ownership model.
2. Research five potential locations for their RV parks.
3. Plan their concessions, when they will need seasonal employees, and so on.

My *Back of the Napkin* book writing Idea was built around this goal-setting process and ninety-day timeline. My macro goal was sell out soon.

My micro goals included the following:

- Hire interns for up to six months, beginning in the summer, to assist and keep me on track.
- Spend four to six hours per week writing content.
- Draft one to two chapters per month with examples and homework.
- Hire a graphic artist professional to pull the project together.
- Hire a smart and ambitious film producer to identify paths to publication.

I got off track when I fell and broke my arm at the end of the summer and couldn't type. I needed to take a break anyway to stay on top of client and family work. So, I shifted my micro goals:

- Hire an intern during January/February.
- Narrow the scope of the book.
- Repurpose some really cool material I had written in the past.
- Get back on track.

Now you are ready to complete your Chapter 3 micro and macro goal worksheet and ninety-day timeline.

CHAPTER 4

Choice of Entity

Your choice of entity will depend on many factors. These include your endgame, your tax situation and the tax position of your investors, your projected profits and losses over the next few years, and your ability to manage complexity of legal compliance. There is no single answer that fits everyone. That said, if you cannot decide what entity to use, I recommend that you default to a limited liability company taxed as a partnership (or disregarded if owned by a single person) because this is the easiest to maintain, most flexible, and has the lowest cost to upgrade or change as you alter your plans.

In choosing an entity, you need three things:

- liability limitation for the owners
- tax efficiency
- ease of operation

Limited Liability

Corporations (including S corporations) provide full liability protection for all owners regardless of the role the owners play in management.

Limited liability companies provide the same full liability protection for owners as corporations.

Limited partnerships provide liability protection to limited partners as long as those partners do not participate actively in management. The general partner has general liability exposure for the debts of the entity. This can create problems when the general partner and one or more of the limited partners are related to each other. For example, if the general partner is owned by Jack and Jill as Jack-Jill Co GP and both Jack and Jill are also investor limited partners and officers, there is a risk that the limited liability will be violated, and Jack and Jill will end up exposed to liability in the same way as the general partner. Today, we use limited partnership for large private funds but not for very much else.

Tax Efficiency

Tax laws change frequently. The following information should be confirmed at the time you make a choice to ensure it is updated. Check with your lawyer and accountant before following this advice.

Limited Liability Companies and Partnerships (Limited and General)

Limited liability companies and their cousins, partnerships, are usually *tax partnerships* if they have more than one owner and *disregarded entities* if they have only one owner. That means the entity reports income and losses to the owners, but the entity itself does not pay taxes. Owners may have different levels of personal income tax rates, so the amount of taxes payable by each owner will vary. But there is never any double taxation.

Tax partnerships can have multiple classes of owners. Owners who contribute funding can be compensated differently from owners who put in talent but not cash. Owners who fund can receive allocations of losses in proportion to their investment (they like this). There are some funky rules about risk-based allocations that your accountant and tax lawyer need to explain to you. But in general, tax partnerships (like LLCs) are the most flexible.

One caveat that catches unwary owners who are also employees: if you own 2 percent or more of a tax partnership, the entity cannot send you a W-2 and cannot pay your FICA, FUTA, and other payroll taxes for you. This trips up some people. There are workarounds that involve some complexity. But be sure that your accountant knows this rule. It can be a mess to restate your tax returns if an accountant or payroll services company lets you issue W-2s to owners.

Corporations: Corporations pay taxes. Shareholders of corporations pay taxes when they receive distributions in the form of dividends or in cashing out their shares. Shareholders who are also employees pay taxes on their salaries. The tax rates at each of these levels changes often. But in the best-case scenario, most shareholders of corporations end up paying taxes *at least twice* on every dollar earned. Sometimes, with small, closely held companies owned by the people who will be the highest paid employees, it makes sense to form a corporation and to zero out the income each year by paying taxable salaries to the owner/employees. But there are limitations on reasonable compensation.

If the company keeps growing, this zero-out strategy will have limits. Also, if the owners plan to sell out, the sales proceeds from an asset sale will be subject to double taxation.

Note that in many businesses, it is uncommon for an exit to be structured as a sale of stock.

However, if the buyer does want to buy equity instead of assets, an acquiring company will not want corporation stock. You will have to pay extra to restructure and will likely have to absorb some double tax costs as a reduction in your purchase price if you try to go into an exit as a corporation.

S Corporations. S corporations do not pay taxes at the entity level. However, there are strict limits on how S corporations can allocate income and losses. If one or more of the founders puts in disproportionate amounts of money, those funding parties will want to take advantage of tax losses/deductions in proportion to their ownership interests. S corporations cannot allow this because they are stuck with a single class of equity. There are other limitations on S corporations that can trip you up. For the most part, only individuals can own them, for example. You need to work closely with your advisers before choosing this kind of entity.

Note that in an exit, an acquiring company will not want S corporation stock. You will have to pay extra to restructure and will likely have to absorb some double tax costs as a reduction to your purchase price if you try to go into an exit as an S corporation.

Warning: Many small-firm accountants will push you toward the kind of entity (often an S corporation) that they understand best. S corporations have significant legal limitations on the types of owners. They can create tax havoc on exit. They are hard to scale as your business needs to grow to include formation of subsidiaries. Choose S corporations wisely and on a limited basis. Typically, I find them most useful for small groups of professionals with equal ownership interests who do not intend to grow beyond five to ten owners. They can also be useful for special purpose management services companies in complex groups of affiliated companies.

Ease of Operation

Corporations have to follow certain legal processes and formalities. They need to have a board of directors and officers (at least three). They must hold annual meetings and elections. They need to keep minutes from their meetings. These are all really important processes in large organizations with many investors and large amounts of funding at stake. But they can be hard to remember and keep up with for smaller companies.

LLCs and partnerships don't have those requirements unless the parties agree to instate them. Normally, the number of required legal hoops (like annual meetings and reports) scales with the size of the company and with the distance between the actual boots on the ground operators and the people putting in the money. If everyone is in the mix of operations and investment all day every day, then the formalities are not very important.

One Last Point

All legal entities require you to adopt a *rule book* for operations. For corporations, the rule books are called bylaws, certificate of formation (sometimes articles of incorporation), shareholders' agreement, and buy-sell agreement. For LLCs and partnerships, the rule books are called company agreements, partnership agreements, or operating agreements and certificate of formation. Collectively, these rule books set out your choices.

This book is about unbundling the complicated legal choices you need to make with your lawyers' help as you put pen to paper on the documents needed to formalize all of your legal relationships.

There is no shortcut to working through the details of your relationships with your cofounders, your management team, your investors, and your Key Contributors.

It may seem easy to buy an off-the-shelf set of bylaws or company agreement documents from an online company or a minute book with canned versions of these documents from an office supply store. But those basic forms will not help you manage the relationships and risks.

At a minimum, you will need legal documents that clearly show what your priorities and preferences are in the following key areas:

- funding (start-up and additional capital)
- tax management
- distribution of cash
- management of day-to-day activities
- voting on big-picture and strategic matters
- removing or adding owners
- buying and selling interest after life events like death, divorce, disability, sales of the company

Regardless of choice of entity, you have to file certificate of formation, adopt your company agreement (bylaws, partnership agreement), get a tax ID number, and open a bank account before you can start.

You have already learned about funding and the management of day-to-day activities and voting. Tax management is beyond the scope of this book. In later chapters, you'll learn about options and tricks to solve the Human Factor of removing or adding owners and other buy-sell events. If you work through the issues, your lawyers can help you put pen to paper on the corporate documents. You will not find an online form that does an adequate job addressing these important issues.

Drafting of comprehensive documents can be done in stages as you grow and add funding and complexity. Work with your lawyer on timelines and budgets. Ask your lawyer hard questions and ask for fixed fees. Make intelligent decisions about what you can defer and what you really should work through now. This book will *save you money*.

> **Camp Car Story**. Alicia and Michelle have the macro goal of selling their enterprise to a larger, national company. Their enterprise will have some employees, some assets (mostly IP and vehicles), and contracts with the owners of RV parks. Any exit they undertake will likely be structured as an *asset sale* and not an *equity sale*—that
> is to say the purchaser will buy their stuff and not their company per se. Purchasers prefer to do asset sales when they can because it allows purchasers to leave behind most hidden liabilities and start fresh with a clean company. But this means that Alicia and Michelle's company, not each of them individually or their investors, will be the seller and will recognize the gain from the sale.
>
> An LLC will give them the liability protection they need, the flexibility to have multiple classes of ownership if they want to raise money or give their employees some share of the equity, and a way to avoid double taxation. Anytime a company plans an asset sale as its exit, an LLC is usually the right way to go.
>
> **Rocket Fuel Story**. The founders of Rocket Fuel also have the macro goal of selling their enterprise. Their valuable assets could be a complex bag of intellectual property, inventory, distribution and/ or manufacturing facilities, and contracts. It's unclear whether they
> will be able to structure an asset sale or will have an equity sale as the proper exit.
>
> It is likely, however, that they will need to raise some significant capital and to accept grants and loans from institutions like Rice University, NASA, or other complicated for-profit, governmental, or nonprofit organizations. They might end up with some foreign investors also, such as the European Space Agency. Some of those types of investors cannot or will not legally invest in LLCs for tax and regulatory reasons.

But on the front end, they want to minimize their taxes, keep their structure simple, and have full liability protection. An LLC is the right kind of entity for them to start with. But they may find that it is necessary to upgrade to a C Corp later as their relationships with bigger institutions evolve.

Diamond Productions Story. Diamond Productions followed the same logic as Alicia and Michelle to form their first company as an LLC. Soon after forming an LLC, they located a large warehouse and shipping complex in East Houston that is eligible for certain tax credits for redevelopment. The space is clean and structurally sound and very cheap. It had been used for event decoration storage, but with the COVID-19 downturn in event planning, the owners are selling it. A Houston-based production company is interested in creating a local sound stage and production studio, but they don't have the capital to fund the whole project. The Houston company is developing a strong reputation for producing LatinX and hip-hop artists in videos and short films. Diamond Productions and the Houston production company spend a few months haggling over a budget and, more specifically, the Decision Matrix on what a joint venture might look like in day-to-day management and strategic terms. Each has a dedicated management team member who is passionate about the project. They decide to form an LLC to legally document their joint venture and fund it with $100,000 each, plus guarantees of a $400,000 bank loan. If they disagree materially on any item, they first bring the disagreement to the Houston Cinema Arts Commission (a nonprofit) to help mediate the dispute. If they still disagree, Diamond Productions has the right to buy out the other party. The JV has a solid business plan, an exit strategy for disputes, a good management team, and meets the long-term objectives of both venturers.

Most early-stage companies will find LLCs fit their start-up needs best. There are exceptions. And tax laws change frequently. Check with your tax advisor *and* your corporate lawyer before you decide on the right form of entity. Sometimes it makes sense to form two or more legal entities to accomplish your goals of risk management, funding, and tax planning. This is not a simple decision. But you can also change your course later as your needs evolve.

CHAPTER 5

Nonprofits and B Corporations

In Chapter 4, we discussed the different types of for-profit legal entities. Many readers may be wondering what type of legal entity is best suited for their nonprofit or hybrid "do well by doing good" venture. Today many entrepreneurs are focusing their energy on building companies that specifically benefit a larger community, beyond the scope of their investors' pocketbooks.

In this chapter, we present two alternative ways to structure ventures for alternative goals: the nonprofit and the B Corp.

B Corporations have real investors who hope to see a return on their investment but are willing to tolerate lower, slower, or different types of returns on those investments in favor of the B Corp's public welfare goals. We'll discuss that in more detail below.

One way to think about a nonprofit is to imagine a company where the *public good* is the investor. Individuals or institutions contribute money to a nonprofit without the expectation of receiving a return on that contribution in the form of profits or other personal benefits. The US taxpayer effectively subsidizes qualifying nonprofits by allowing them to conduct some or all of their activities without paying taxes. So, the *public*, in the form of contributors and taxpayers, is the investor.

To become a nonprofit, the founders need to follow the same basic steps as an LLC or corporation. But there are two key differences in the formation documents and some extra steps required to obtain tax-exempt status.

The nonprofit purpose. The nonprofit purpose is a key part of the certificate of formation and the bylaws. Before drafting your purpose statement, make sure you consult with your tax adviser about what category of nonprofit you will be for IRS purposes. The language you use in describing your purpose can make or break your application (see 1023 below).

The board. Since a nonprofit doesn't have shareholders or owners, the process of appointing, removing, replacing, and rotating board members becomes more complicated. It is beyond the scope of this book to get into the different choices that might make sense for managing the board appointments. But these are critical parts of setting up good governance and for setting up your entity for compliance with state law and tax law in the future.

File a 1023 to qualify as a nonprofit for federal income tax purposes. See the following pages. This can take months, even a year or more just to prepare the application and can take up to five years to qualify, come off probation, and establish solid practices around filing tax reports and information reports. Be prepared. Be thorough. Find an experienced adviser. Don't be afraid to ask for help.

In an earlier chapter, you learned about raising capital. One of the key takeaways from that chapter is that the securities laws require companies to make meaningful and complete disclosures of their business plans, financial forecasts, biographies of key players, risks, and other factors when raising money from others. The same is generally true of nonprofits. But instead of raising money from private investors, the nonprofit is raising money in the form of tax subsidies from the federal government.

The IRS gathers this information to determine whether your nonprofit should be granted tax-exempt status; (501(c)(3) or 501(c)(4) are the most common designations. The process is not easy for small organizations. But the government does try to help with pretty extensive online materials about how to fill out forms and make the applications. That said, I always recommend that you work carefully with both an experienced lawyer and accountant who have shepherded nonprofits through the process in the past. It is easy to get tripped up on the nuances and the qualifications. Be particularly careful if all or most of your funding will come from a single, private source or a small group of private families. In short, don't just use an online service or do it by yourself. I regularly refer nonprofit clients to unitedway.org for more educational information—and in some cities, the United Way conducts inexpensive seminars for local nonprofits. Also don't be afraid to spend time at https://www.irs.gov/charities-non-profits/applying-for-tax-exempt-status.

Operate within the boundaries that you committed to follow when you qualified at the state and federal level as a nonprofit.

1. Be diligent about tax and informational public reporting.
2. Be diligent about how you raise money and from whom.

Even after your nonprofit obtains tax-exempt status, some of its activities may still be taxable. For example, if the nonprofit owns a building and rents out part of it to a third party, the rents will likely be taxable. Certain kinds of fundraising actually constitute taxable activities. So be careful and surround yourself with experts.

Note that private donors (particularly large ones) will also act like investors and will want seats on the board, regular and thorough information about the finances and operations, and some transparency about governance, goals, and direction. A well-known example of this is the Bill & Melinda Gates Foundation and its investment in hundreds of smaller nonprofits around the world. In my experience, the discipline and oversight provided by sophisticated benefactors is very helpful for smaller nonprofits in helping them grow into the financial and business planning discipline needed to succeed.

> **Nonprofit Story.** Trevor and Diane are freelance social media influencers who travel around the world posting about their adventures. They have a sizable following on YouTube and other outlets and manage to support their travel budgets and also save a bit of money from their ad revenues. They spend part of each year with some indigenous villages in Ecuador and have become fascinated by the craftsmanship around the blankets made from alpaca wool. But they are concerned about literacy and access to health care for the women and children of the villages. They would like to support the villages by asking their followers to make donations to a new nonprofit they are founding. Donors at a certain threshold level of donations ($500?) would receive a blanket.

> My first advice to Trevor and Diane is to do deep and wide research around other US and United Nations and global nonprofits who may be working toward similar

goals in the region. It is expensive and time-consuming to form and operate a new entity. It is easier to tag along with another symbiotic group and help them expand their mission through your influence and leadership.

If there is not a group that meets the needs, then consider applying for a grant from another nonprofit and build on that process. Meanwhile, find a partner who will have the time and energy to dedicate specifically to organizing, qualifying, and maintaining the nonprofit. The first few chapters of this book apply to nonprofits: build a team, set your goals, figure out your funding. Do these things *before* launching the new venture.

If Trevor and Diane still are determined and now prepared to form a nonprofit, they should take some classes and build a board of directors. Hire a lawyer and an accountant. Be patient. Know that this venture will require the same kind of time and energy as any other start-up and may interfere with their focus on their travel adventures.

As a footnote, giving blankets to key donors may or may not be a great idea. Donors may be limited on the tax deductions they can take for donating if they receive a valuable blanket in return for their donation. And, depending on the scope of the blanket business, the whole activity involving blankets may be a for-profit and taxable enterprise even if Trevor and Diane qualify their nonprofit as a charity.

Diamond Productions Story. Diamond Productions premiered its first film at Sundance and landed an international distribution deal. When the founders first launched the company, they committed to giving back both by supporting historically underrepresented writers, producers, directors, and stories but also by creating a pipeline  of young talent. With some of the profits from the first real hit, they decide to set up a foundation to provide scholarships in the amount of $25,000 to two aspiring film students enrolled in accredited universities each year. They create a business and financial plan. They select a board that includes not only the Diamond Productions founders but also some strong role models with deep filmmaking resumes. They hire a part-time director to screen applicants and create a process for selecting winners of the scholarships. After forming a nonprofit under California state law, they begin the process of applying for tax-exempt status with the IRS. The process takes almost two years. But in the end, they qualify as a private foundation.

B Corporation / Public Benefit Corporation

What Is a B Corporation?

It is a company (can be an LLC or a corporation) that elects to adopt and live by values beyond maximizing shareholder profit.

The world is beginning to recognize that there are other very important public and private stakeholders in our economy who can be neglected if shareholder value is the only important value. These silent stakeholders are silent no more and include the following:

- *employees:* a fair wage, a safe workplace, benefits, paid leave, opportunities to advance, job security
- *environment:* reduce, reuse, recycle; minimize greenhouse gas emissions; take care of Mother Earth; don't pollute
- *community:* create jobs and training programs, support local charities, get involved with local schools and government, actively take steps to minimize the company's negative impact on transportation, housing accessibility, parks, and health

These are just a few of the possible stakeholders who might claim a seat at the table and even a piece of the pie in a B corporation.

Why is this a change?

Since the age of the Dutch East India Company and the original corporations, the responsibility of the board and officers of corporations has been maximizing shareholder profits. As long as an action was not illegal, if it maximized shareholders' profits, it was generally tolerated and, in most cases, encouraged. Officers (often rewarded with equity themselves) were single-mindedly focused on keeping the price of stock as high as possible and/or making dividend distributions for the benefit of shareholders.

For public companies today, maximizing shareholder profit is the law of the land. Private companies may adopt more flexible and inclusive goals. But public companies are held to the standards of state law that impose a very high standard of care on directors and officers as guardians of shareholders' profits. Shareholder lawsuits are an effective tool—even if only as a threat—to prevent public companies from elevating stakeholders (employees, environment, community) to the same level as shareholders.

So, B corporation statutes are a meaningful and necessary tool to allow public companies to broaden their missions.

> **Lemonade—A Real-Life Example**. It makes economic sense. In 2020, the first B corporation made an IPO or initial public offering and became a publicly traded stock on the New York Stock Exchange: Lemonade, an insurance company targeting millennials, initially priced their stock at $27/share and on the first day of the offering, the price increased 140 percent. Lemonade's socially conscious goal is called "Give Back," and they donate a percentage of profits to a portfolio of charitable causes. It is not clear whether worker benefits or other "social goods" are also part of

the B Corp mission of Lemonade. Maybe it is enough to commit to dedicate profits
to recognized charities.

The stated good was *not just* shareholder value but also paying it forward by making a clear commitment to funding designated nonprofits.

How do we hold B Corps accountable?

Great question. Many companies make promises to protect their employees, the environment, and
communities. And those promises help them get access to resources like lower taxes in cities bidding
to have them move in and create jobs. But who actually monitors this stuff?

B-Lab is a private bank that lends money to B corporations but also provides an annual certifi-
cation process. B Corps must walk the walk, not just talk the talk, if they want to keep their certifications. The process is not foolproof. But since money is attached (loans), certified companies have
an incentive to play the game.

This is a new system. And it is a private, not public system. Our legal system evolves more slowly
than our economy, and government regulations and standards for a new kid on the block like a B
Corp are possibly decades away.

It is important to note that the tax status of an enterprise is not impacted by its B Corp status.
That means the IRS really does not have any role at all in enforcement.

B Corps are operating outside of this existing infrastructure of accountability in many ways,
given that they are a rather recent development by legal standards. Time will tell whether the private
certifications and continuous monitoring by the third-party B-Lab will be sufficient to create a reliable culture of compliance that the public, the shareholders, the employees, and others really trust.

This is another way of saying that our economy hasn't yet experienced its first big, public, expensive B Corp scandal.

So, should you elect to become a B Corp?

It depends.

There are many ways to make the world a better place. If you are a small, private company, you
may want to just structure your business in a way that makes you and your investors and employees
proud.

You may be maximizing shareholder/investor value already by attracting better employees with
family-friendly policies or by obtaining property tax benefits from the city with a promise to develop
a park or create new jobs.

And your investors may make the credible argument that if you earn money for them, you are
empowering them to make larger contributions to charities that can leverage their skills even more
efficiently than your small company can in improving public welfare.

However, there is value in a brand. Some smaller brands are adopting B Corp status and brag-
ging about it to their target customers. If millennials and their younger siblings jump on the B Corp
bandwagon, it may be worth it for the older generations who are still providing the capital for growth
to agree to a B Corp structure for private company investments.

Some industries (ice cream, anyone?) have some leading players who are B Corps. This may create
pressure for others in the same space to also become B Corps.

Jenni's Splendid Ice Cream Story. Known for their delicious artisanal ice cream, Jenni's has gained popularity for their natural flavors. All of their desserts are made from milk sourced from a farm in the Appalachia region of Ohio that has been in the family for many years. Using natural milk proteins over added stabilizers not only makes their ice cream delicious, but it also has the benefit of promoting Jenni's as a company that is doing good. In addition, Jenni's advertises the use of direct trade ingredients, a diverse employment team, and their relationships with women and minority-owned businesses. Their B-Corp status lends immense value to the Jenni's brand, presenting them as a company that is evolving for a better world.

Diamond Productions Story. Christine, Elara, and Tomas are considering electing for B Corp status for their company Diamond Productions. As experienced filmmakers each with individual success, they want to pay it forward by nurturing the filmmaking careers of minority filmmakers. They are not necessarily bound by  money; they choose films because they see something in the filmmaker or feel the story needs to be told—documentaries, moving stories, and so on. Becoming a B Corp would highlight their dual goals of helping others and making money. The founders are still working with their attorneys on whether a C Corp or an LLC makes the most sense for them. If they elect to become an LLC, they will not need to formally become a B Corp but can incorporate some of the same public service goals into their company agreement.

Conclusion

Use the homework to evaluate whether your goals fit best with a nonprofit, a B Corp, or just a very well-focused LLC.

Keep in mind that a nonprofit must comply with state and federal tax and corporate governance laws because they are taking funds for the benefit of the public. This can be burdensome. The cost of tax compliance is high. And many founders are just not ready for the type of formalities and discipline required to really comply with the public trust requirements.

B corporations ultimately are corporations. They report to shareholders. Many are public companies with the threat of shareholder lawsuits hanging over their heads if their focus drifts from the traditional corporate purpose of maximizing profits. If your company does not need to be a corporation for raising capital or tax-planning purposes, it may be overkill to adopt the corporate form just to make a B Corp election.

Finally, the versatile LLC format allows owners of private companies to contractually agree to adopt principles and goals that lift up employees, or the environment, or cows, or scientific research, or other quasi-nonprofit goals. Our country honors those private contracts even if they result in a lower profit return calculus in the end.

CHAPTER 6

Key Contracts

Essentially, each chapter of this book is a mini lesson on block and tackling the fundamentals of the contracts you will negotiate to document your legal relationships.

Foundational Contracts

Contracts among the founders and investors are your foundational documents, and together with ongoing revisions to these contracts and written records of your big and important decisions (resolutions), they make up your corporate records, often called your minute book. You will put these contracts in a drawer and forget about them until you need more money, have a dispute with an investor or other owner, need to follow through on a buy-sell event, or need a refresher on who needs to vote on what kinds of decisions (Decision Matrix). You will need these documents kept current for a sale. And anyone who comes along in the future to buy or invest in the company will want to see that you have good foundational contracts.

Operational Contracts:

- employment and independent contractor agreements
- leases
- licenses
- distribution agreements
- IP agreements
- nondisclosure agreements (NDAs)
- term sheets or letters of intent (LOIs)
- purchase orders
- standard terms and conditions
- master sales/services agreements
- loans

Drafting and Negotiating

Depending on the type of business you have, it may make sense for you to work with your lawyer to develop your own templates or base forms for your commonly used contracts. This is particularly true if you are providing goods or services to consumers (retail businesses) or to other smaller businesses (B2B). Spending time and money developing agreements that protect your rights, clearly spell out the terms of the transaction, and assign risks prevents litigation later. A handshake is rarely the right answer. An exchange of emails/texts/WhatsApp messages is roughly equivalent to a handshake.

If your business is just starting or if you regularly provide goods or services to much larger companies, you will likely be required to sign the other party's contracts. You might freak out the first time your dream customer sends you a ninety-page, 10-point type standard form. But don't despair. Many of the provisions in the standard form likely do not apply to you. And many clauses are quite easy to negotiate to make agreements more balanced and fairer. A good lawyer can save you time, money, and risk by helping you identify what can and cannot be negotiated, what is unfair, and what is going to be a hidden cost to the deal. The Serenity Prayer comes to mind …

> Grant me the patience to accept the things I cannot change;
> the courage to change the things I can;
> and the wisdom to know the difference.

In the context of legal agreements, your lawyer can provide patience, courage, and wisdom.

Before you hire a lawyer, it makes sense to understand the basic vocabulary around some common clauses. Consider the next section to be like SAT exam prep. Learn these terms, and both meetings with your lawyer and contracts will seem less daunting.

Common Contract Clauses

ADA means the Americans with Disabilities Act.

Arbitration along with **mediation** are two forms of alternative dispute resolution. If a contract contains these clauses, you likely cannot sue in a court of law for damages. Instead, you are required to resolve disputes through the private arbitration or mediation processes set out in the contract.

Consideration is a fancy legal term for "What do I get?" The first day of law school, lawyers learn that there is only a binding legal contract if each party actually agrees to both give something and get something. If I promise to give you a diamond ring tomorrow, this is *not* a contract because it is unclear what I get. If I promise to give you a diamond ring tomorrow in exchange for tickets to the Super Bowl, there is a contract because each party is both giving and getting. Note that the word *consideration* is rarely used in contracts. But the concept is essential.

Jury trial waiver is common in commercial contracts and basically means a judge, not a jury, will try any case arising under the contract.

Purchase order refers to the summary of business terms often found in an email attachment, a form on a website, or an attachment to a longer document. Note that purchase orders almost always make reference to *terms and conditions*. If you haven't read the terms and conditions, you really don't know what you are signing.

Terms and conditions mean the background legal document sometimes hidden in a tab on a website that sets out very important legal conditions that govern every commercial transaction between the parties, including many of the clauses described in this chapter. Read it.

Term refers to how long the parties are committed to perform under the contract. It is common to have commercial contracts that last one, three, five, or more years. But it is also very common to have exceptions to the stated term, allowing one or both parties to get out of it with notice and possibly the payment of a penalty. Leases, licenses, NDAs, and joint ventures typically are the hardest to terminate early. Sales of goods and services, employment agreements, and specialty contracts commonly have early termination options.

Incoterms refers to an international set of prenegotiated standards for assigning risk and costs to the shipping and delivery of goods cross border. If you are buying a container of your product from China, you need to understand the Incoterms referenced in the agreement, so you know where the Chinese manufacturer's responsibility ends and your starts.

Indemnification clauses are among the most important clauses in contracts for the sale of goods or services in an environment where human life is at risk or there are mutual risks from performance of the services. Both parties are interested in clarity about who must pay for what damages. These are complicated clauses. In most cases, they should be mutual or reciprocal. Sometimes they are completely unenforceable under the laws of a particular state. *Do not assume these clauses are fair or enforceable.* Pay your lawyer to negotiate these.

The UCC (see glossary) governs the basic framework of almost all sales of goods between a buyer and seller. If there are no written terms of the sale, the default rules are the UCC rules in domestic contracts between US buyers and sellers. Think of the UCC as the backup terms and conditions for the domestic sale of goods, the payment of invoices, and the collection of debts where there are no overriding written agreements. The UCC does other things too, like make it possible to obtain a security interest when you loan money.

Force majeure clauses are sometimes called "Act of God" exemptions and include a way for the parties to defer, delay, or cancel their obligations under the contract or to reprice their deliverables in the context of very unusual (and generally unforeseeable) circumstances. The law in this area is evolving rapidly, and all clauses should be reviewed and revised in light of the unprecedented business interruptions caused by the COVID-19 pandemic. Global warming events are also changing the way force majeure is used. And in some countries, labor disruptions can be considered force majeure events.

Law Firm Story. Shayla, Jorge, and Maggie choose Shayla to figure out the ins and outs of signing a lease for their new law firm. Shayla hires a commercial real estate agent who tries to convince them to take on 10,000 square feet of class A space in a prime downtown area on the thirty-second floor with a view and a big conference room. Shayla knows that the real estate agent is compensated by the  landlord on commission and is skeptical about taking on so much space, especially when she finds out that they would have to each sign as personal guarantors. Shayla uses the checklist in this book to review the proposed lease. The allowances for build-out are not great. The law firm would have to commit to a minimum of sixty months. No subleases are allowed without landlord consent. There is a shared services fee for the building's common areas, and the price of parking is not capped. When she considers the cost of furnishings, copier leases, and a receptionist, the whole package looks like a big deal for a start-up. Reading the lease for the fine print helped Shayla uncover the additional costs and risks. In the end, the new firm decided to take offices in a shared space location where each could have a private office, they have access to a conference room, and the public amenities like the lunchroom and reception are included. It is not quite as nice as the cool class A building. But they signed a one-year agreement with no hidden costs and are more comfortable with the budget.

Camp Car Story. Alicia and Michelle's first order of business is to buy or develop tracking software to make it easy to rent, track, and recover their rent cars. They know that LIME scooters and Zip Car already have software that performs similar tracking functions. But they aren't sure if that software is proprietary to those companies, can be licensed, or must be developed independently. Since neither Alicia nor Michelle is a tech geek, they decide to hire a former UBER developer, Jess, to present some options to them for the software development. They put Jess to work under an independent contractor agreement. Jess comes back in a month and recommends that they develop their own software and use an offshore company out of Mexico City to do the development work. Now they need a software development agreement that not only lays out the scope of work but also handles the international aspect of the deal. They fill out the who, what, when, where, why, and how much homework and go to their corporate lawyer, who refers them to her licensing and tech partner. They paper the deal and are very happy that they spent the money to define the terms well. Next, Alicia and Michelle need a website. They could start with a simple online web design platform. But instead, they engage a marketing/social media firm to advise them on how best to reach their targets. The marketing company has its own engagement letter. Before signing that letter, the founders map out their objectives clearly using the who, what, when, where, why, and how much formula. They then engage their licensing lawyer to review the engagement letter and tweak it to clarify some of the more vague provisions and add an indemnification clause. The lawyer's work costs about $500, which is money well spent when the marketing firm switches out personnel on their project and they need to challenge their rights six months later.

Rocket Fuel Story. After stubbing their toes on the complexity of export regulations, the leadership team of Rocket Fuel decides to take try different tactic. They did some homework through one of their major feed stock suppliers to find out how other chemical and fuel companies reach foreign markets. Part of the homework con-  sisted of identifying their own needs—the who, what, when, where, why, how much checklist.

Then they interviewed three international specialty distributors with global expertise in chemical sales. They targeted the European and Japanese markets with their nascent private rocket companies, and they engaged two different distributors: one for Europe and one for Asia. It was tricky to negotiate commissions. And a primary goal was to avoid having to figure out the import and export complexities, so they needed companies with great depth of experience in that area. They engaged both a seasoned international lawyer and a customs lawyer to help negotiate the distribution agreements. They ran extensive background and reference checks on the distributors. And they started with a few small orders.

Over time, Rocket Fuel became more comfortable selling into the EU markets but did not really gain traction in Japan. They terminated the Asian distributor's contract by giving notice and settling existing accounts. And they formed a legal subsidiary in Belgium. The legal subsidiary helped with tax planning but added complexity when they entertained bids for an exit several years later.

CHAPTER 7

Customers and Suppliers

The most important rule about customers is that you need them. The greatest idea is just an idea until someone will buy it.

The second is the 80/20 rule that says 80 percent of your business will likely come from 20 percent of your customers. Take good care of those 20 percent and see if you can minimize the resources you allocate to the 80 percent to grow your business efficiently.

What does your lawyer want you to know about customers?

You need to have written contracts that accomplish your real business goals. Downloading forms off the internet will not necessarily align your relationship with your customers. The customer homework found in the back of this book will help you decide what kind of relationships you have.

Your lawyer also wants you and your sales team to understand the basics of contracts. So, let's play the doughnut game:

A true contract has three parts: offer, acceptance, consideration.

If you are missing any of these parts, then the contract is not binding on either party. Try this game to see if you can identify the missing parts. How does the offer/counteroffer process get in the way of a true offer, acceptance, consideration model?

Buy a dozen doughnuts and bring in some poker chips to play the game over coffee with your sales team.

Offer	Counteroffer	Action/Counteroffer	Do You Have a Contract?	Notes
Offer to deliver a doughnut tomorrow to Jim for two chips.	Jim says he'll buy it for one chip tomorrow and two chips today.	You hand Jim a doughnut today.	No	Jim does not have to pay but cannot eat the doughnut.
Offer to sell three doughnuts to Jessica for six chips.	Jessica agrees to buy two doughnuts for three chips.	You agree to sell two plain doughnuts for three chips but need four chips for filled doughnuts.	Maybe	It depends on whether Jessica wants plain or filled.
Offer to sell the whole box of doughnuts to Jamal for ten chips.	Jamal accepts but says he will have to pay you on Tuesday.	You agree to accept payment on Tuesday.	Yes	Offer, counteroffer, acceptance, consideration
Offer to sell the whole box of doughnuts to Jasmine for ten chips.	Jasmine accepts and pays you ten chips but says you need to deliver the doughnuts to her daughter's kindergarten class two miles away by 11:00 a.m.	You don't have a delivery person available and refuse the condition.	No	Offer, counteroffer, rejection
Offer to sell two doughnuts selected by Jared to Jared for three chips.	Jared agrees and picks two filled doughnuts.	Jared requests that you guarantee that the two filled doughnuts are one lemon and one strawberry.	Probably	By allowing Jared to select his own, there is likely an implied guaranty that the flavors are what they seem.

The doughnut game shows you that common business transactions can be really confusing. Offers, counteroffers, counter-counteroffers, and so on can hide the original terms and make it difficult to tell what either party has agreed to do.

Many times, a seller's offer says "subject to seller's terms and conditions" set out below. Buyer accepts the contract with a confirmation, but the confirmation has fine print that says, "subject to buyer's terms and conditions." If the buyer pays and the seller delivers, seller has effectively agreed to buyer's terms and conditions.

Morals of the Story

1. Don't agree to terms and conditions you don't understand.
2. Educate your sales team on what they can and can't accept.
3. Develop your own preferred terms and conditions and a parallel checklist of preferred positions so you know how to evaluate what a customer requests against what you realistically want to sell.

Your lawyer wants you to know basic contract principals and to have a preferred position on each of them.

Before you sign anything, make sure you fully understand all these terms. They may be in fine print. They may be in big bold letters. They are definitely confusing and boring. But you need to work with your lawyer to understand them in each deal you undertake.

What is a mutual indemnity?

What is a warranty for fitness of purpose?

What is a most favored nations clause?

What does force majeure mean, and does it normally include global pandemics or hurricanes?

What is a nonsolicitation clause?

What is the normal, enforceable term for a nondisclosure agreement?

Can you terminate a contract by sending an email?

Your lawyer wants you to know that even if you are David negotiating with Goliath, you can and should still read the fine print, understand the contract, and ask for what you want.

If your customers are gigantic companies who have their own contracts, it is still worth it to have a lawyer work with you to review and understand those agreements. Even the most impenetrable, ninety-page agreements *are negotiable* on key terms. Plus, you need to make sure the business terms are set out correctly. An experienced lawyer can be on retainer for a two- three-hour review/advise project to point out what you should change and what you realistically can change in these monster contracts, and to coach you in how to get the changes you need.

> **Story of the Big, Bad Drilling Company.** Once upon a time, a giant energy exploration and production company (Big Driller) wanted to buy engineering services from Little Supplier to be delivered by a team of smart engineers on an offshore platform in the Gulf of Mexico. Now this kind of contract is for very important services in a risky environment where absolute expertise and perfection are required to prevent really bad stuff from happening (remember Deepwater Horizon?). This kind of contract gets negotiated daily in Houston, and the industry has developed some market standards for how to balance the allocation risks between Big Driller and Little Supplier. And Little Supplier was smart enough to call their lawyer to ask for help negotiating the contract.
>
> But Big Driller's contract was *out of market*, which is lawyer-speak for really, really overreaching. It shifted the risk of safety around the engineers' lives to Little Supplier even while the engineers were on the platform under the supervision of Big Driller. It shifted the risk of product failure completely to Little Supplier even if Big Driller's

other integrated people and products were substandard in their performance. In short, Big Driller's contract dealt Little Supplier a raw deal.

Little Supplier's lawyer reviewed the contract and advised Little Supplier to negotiate for knock-for-knock indemnity clauses, mutual releases, various worker protections, and liability shifts. Little Supplier tried hard to get Big Driller to bend to the market standards, but Big Driller stood firm.

Little Supplier went back over and over again with reasonable requests that peers to Big Driller would normally accept, and Big Driller would not bend.

Little Supplier's lawyer finally advised Little Supplier that the UCC and the Texas common law of contracts offered more protection than the written contract. After consulting with Little Supplier's insurance carrier about coverage, Little Supplier agreed to do the work *with no written agreement*. Big Driller was desperate to get the engineers on board and agreed, or sort of slipped it by without letting their lawyers know.

This was a happily ever after story. No one died. The work and products installed were of excellent quality, and there were no issues. But in reality, if the project had been Deepwater Horizon, the blowup and lawsuits that followed could have bankrupted Little Supplier.

This was the only time in the author's thirty-year career that she advised a client to do any significant and risky work without a written contract.

Customers and Suppliers

The old saying "a customer is always right" can bankrupt your business. Customer service is important. But defining the terms of your obligations to a customer is very important. From the smallest retail shop to the largest industrial supplier or web-based behemoth, the seller must set boundaries and rules around its customer transactions. Maybe the rules are posted on a blackboard behind the register and say, "No Returns without a Receipt." Maybe the rules are part of a twenty-page click-through terms and conditions link on a website or ap. Either way, define your boundaries clearly and visibly for your customers.

Suppliers are like customers in reverse. When you are the customer, the other party is the supplier. You want the best terms for purchasing goods or services. The supplier may have standard terms and conditions that they prefer to apply to all their customers. Sometimes when you are buying commodity goods or services, like paper at the office supply shop or a copier for the office or software as a service contract from a vendor like Microsoft, you just take the terms they offer. But often, you can and should negotiate—even with your lawyer.

Before you create your form of customer contract or sign a supply contract, do your homework to clarify your objectives. Then make sure you have answers in writing in the final contract to all of the ten basic terms below:

Ten Terms for All Contracts

- Who?
- What?
- When?
- Where?
- How Many?
- Price?
- Terms of Delivery?
- What warranties are appropriate (and return policy)?
- What are the policies for cancellation?
- Choice of law and dispute procedures?

Know when there is an actual, enforceable contract (review the doughnut game). Don't agree to buy or sell anything on a handshake. And never agree to the standard terms and conditions found on a website without really understanding them. Of course, if you are buying stock goods from a major manufacturer, you may not have the ability to negotiate. But in most cases where you are buying any kind of custom goods, services, or creative products, you can and indeed *should* negotiate.

As always, *please* consult your lawyer before signing any kind of contract that is large enough for you to put people, important resources, or significant money at risk.

Special Terms for Services Contracts

- staffing requirements and qualifications
- hourly rates of staff
- right to substitute staff
- safety or licensing of personnel
- indemnification for breach
- indemnification for harm or injury to supplier personnel who go on site to your place of business
- insurance requirements
- no-hire clauses (preventing the buyer from poaching the personnel of the service provider)

Special Terms for Software Development or Similar Custom Creative Work Contracts

- work-for-hire clauses
- ownership of work product
- permitted and/or prohibited inclusion of third-party or free/open-source software
- security
- privacy

- minimum performance requirements
- licenses and rights to use intellectual property belonging to other parties

Rocket Fuel Story. Luke, Anakin, and Sally are looking at purchasing engineering services for the ongoing construction of a building for their rocket fuel company, Company XYX.

Here, their general contractor needs to hire a specialized engineering team to conduct stress testing on concrete foundations in their building, which is currently under construction. The contractor puts the project out to bid and selects a structural engineering company. The engineering company has hired several summer interns from a local university and has recently had some retirements of key, seasoned engineers. The general contractor does not specify who the project team should be, and the engineering company staffs it heavily with summer interns supervised by relatively junior staff engineers. On site one day, a summer intern gets hit in the head by a forklift and is not wearing a helmet or safety vest at the time of the accident. The project comes in late. The documentation is inadequate and not descriptive enough for the general contractor's purposes. The summer intern suffers a concussion and sues the general contractor as well as the engineering company for unsafe work environment. OSHA comes in to investigate. It is a big, expensive mess. The contract is really only a purchase order. And the engineering company's insurance is refusing to pay. What went wrong for Luke, Anakin, and Sally—and why?

Types of Contracts

A **lease** is a specialized and common form of a supply contract. A checklist for leases is in the homework for this chapter.

A **distribution agreement** is an agreement for one party to serve as an intermediary sales agent for a manufacturer. A checklist for distribution agreements is in the homework for this chapter.

A **license** is a very technical, specialized form of supply contract. You can think of a license as a form of a lease, but instead of real estate or equipment, the lease is for intellectual property.

An **independent contractor agreement** is another specialized form of supply contract (sometimes called an agency or services agreement) discussed in the next chapter.

Did you know that your **engagement letter** with your lawyer or accountant is a form of supply contract and a form of an independent contractor agreement? Even though these may look like letters, they should always have the standard terms and address the ten terms. Get clarity on all these points even when negotiating with your own lawyer!

Don't be afraid to negotiate. Even the monster contracts can be negotiated on important points.

CHAPTER 8
Employees and Contractors

Most successful entrepreneurs have the gift of persuading others to help in the cause of building the business. The enthusiasm, optimism, and vision of start-up founders is infectious often in a very good way. Colleagues, friends, family members, and others jump in on the project, lending small and large resources to the cause.

Sometimes all these contributors need or want is a thank you! For them, the sincere gratitude, and the feeling of being part of something big is important.

But more commonly, you need to compensate your support team and at the same time protect your business.

The trickiest supporters are those who *create intellectual property* and *existing employees*. We'll handle each of those separately below.

I'll Pay You Tomorrow—Sorting out the Key Contributors of Value

For now, your homework is to fill out the time and talent survey in the homework section and sort your Key Contributors into three groups: green, yellow, and red.

The *green category* consists of one-time contributors of something with a readily defined value. This includes free rent, free equipment, consulting on developing a business plan, legal services, and other helpful people who do a defined job on an infrequently referring basis.

Once you've identified the green category, pay them something in cash and separate ties. Don't forget the assignment of rights if they have helped with any intellectual property.

The *yellow category* includes those providing recurring services, long-term benefits, and very important connections. These may be existing employees or independent contractors or providers of some other kind of in-kind value. They don't deserve or want a seat at the Founders' Table. But they really identify as mission critical players on your team. They may not have quit their day jobs, but they have sacrificed some evenings and weekends or turned down other work to join your team. You need them, and they believe in you.

For the yellow category, get a consulting agreement or other relevant contract in place (lease, loan, etc.). Figure out how to pay them some cash each month and don't dig a hole that is too deep. Make sure your work with both your tax adviser and a lawyer if you offer up equity. There are many ways to do that, and all of them are complicated and have tax implications.

Often your yellow category creates intellectual property—including brand, logo, training materials, business processes, recipes, software, *great ideas*, and similar intangibles. If that is the case—or if there is any question about whether it is the case—put in place an assignment of rights agreement as part of your contract (keep reading for more information about protection of intellectual property).

The *red category* is made up of members of the yellow category who are more intensely involved and committed. These people may have quit their jobs and started working for you without pay. They may have cashed in some of their 401(k) to help you or signed a personal guaranty on your lease. They are followers who have written themselves (with your encouragement or not) into the narrative of the creation of the company.

For the red category, go back to the founders' homework. Is there a way that these red contributors could think they are already part of the founders' team? You need to work with your lawyers to clean up these relationships sooner rather than later. If you do choose to issue them equity, do it with care and keep the tax and balance-of-power issues in mind.

Follow all the steps you would follow for a yellow category supporter at a very minimum. But keep your antenna tuned to the vocabulary and actions that these red category members use internally and externally to describe their roles.

Employees versus Contractors

In the homework for this chapter, you'll find a checklist you can use to determine whether an individual is an employee or an independent contractor, and you'll find some short checklists for the type of information needed for contracts for each party.

Why do I care?

This is a big issue with hidden financial and tax consequences you may not understand until after the misclassification has been in place for a while. Like many issues, there are two parts to the problem: the state/federal law and the tax law issues.

State/federal law. For state/federal law purposes, employers are required to pay into the state's unemployment insurance fund and provide certain minimum benefits (like the FMLA). There are wrongful termination and antidiscrimination rules at the state and federal levels. Worker status (documented vs. undocumented) and right-to-work protections apply to employees, not contractors.

Independent contractors are not protected in the same way.

State budgets are regularly stretched to the limit trying to fund unemployment claims. Often a person will start a complaint about misclassification by filing an unemployment claim. The state then checks to see if this person was, indeed, classified as an employee. If *not*, then an inquiry is opened against the company to determine whether the person was misclassified. This process can also start because of a wrongful termination claim or a discrimination claim.

Tax law. An employer must file and pay payroll taxes, including the employer portion of FICA, FUTA, and Social Security.

A company does not pay taxes on independent contractors. It is the independent contractor's responsibility to pay his or her portion *and* what would normally be the company's portion in an employment scenario. That means independent contractors are supposed to file and pay quarterly estimates with the IRS of taxes they owe. Many are not sophisticated enough or good enough at money management to do this. Some may not realize that the company is not withholding taxes. Put in place a written agreement clearly stating the status of an independent contract and make sure the contract states that the company is *not* paying taxes for the contractor.

The IRS standard for who is an employee versus an independent contractor is a little bit different from most state statutes. In fact, the IRS is more generous in most cases about classifying a person as a contractor as long as the contractor is actually paying into the system.

However, the IRS reports all misclassifications to the state. And some states use the IRS list as their helpful cheat sheet for knowing who to audit.

Diamond Productions Story. Diamond Productions ended up in a lawsuit over misclassification of some of the production assistants working on set for one of their films. Jimmy was a clever and helpful young filmmaker eager to prove his worth. He signed on to Christine's first film with Diamond Productions as a production assistant under a standard independent contractor contract. He was so useful that Christine started using him for back-office work, field development work, and reading scripts to give her a millennial's perspective. His original job of PA on a specific film expanded to a full-time position with Diamond Productions. But Diamond Productions did not put him on payroll. His job description was rather loosely defined. And he worked on a biweekly fixed payment plan without insurance, overtime, or tax withholding. Often, he worked sixty hours or more per week on special projects. Jimmy eventually took a position with Disney and learned that others like him were employees and received payment for overtime and other benefits. His buddy, a labor lawyer, filed a suit on Jimmy's behalf to recover the lost overtime and damages. It was a mess and cost the company much more than it imagined just to get out of the litigation. Then the IRS audited Diamond Productions on underpayment of payroll issues. It took two years and more than $15,000 (in addition to what they had to pay Jimmy) to sort it all out.

Conclusion

In Chapter 1, you put together a strong leadership team. As your company becomes more of an enterprise and less of an abstract idea, the team grows larger. First, sort out whether key players are green—contractors and short-term service employees; yellow—long-term key players; or red—core contributors who might see themselves as founders. For the green (and possibly yellow) category, work through the homework to determine whether an employment or independent contractor relationship is appropriate.

There are complexities to complying with employment law beyond tax compliance. For many companies, the painful experience of a first lawsuit comes because of failure to understand labor and employment law. Don't wing it. Don't rely on an outsourced payroll group to provide legal advice. Spend some time and money on good systems and processes for managing your people, and you will reap the rewards.

CHAPTER 9

Regulatory Issues and the Government's Role in Your Business

From nail salons to real estate to manufacturing and software companies, the local, state, and federal government will have rules governing your activities. Even mom-and-pop toy stores will have to comply with the Americans with Disabilities Act, along with labor and employment rules. We are building businesses in the freest economy in the world, but there are traps everywhere.

You *need* to know the law.

Some regulatory regimes are well known and intuitive, and others are more hidden and industry specific. The following is *not* a comprehensive list. But it should get you thinking.

Environmental law. If you are buying an office building or land, you probably know that you need to investigate the environmental hazards that might come with the purchase. But did you know that long-term tenants can also be tagged with environmental cleanup responsibility in some circumstances, and that tenants must comply with local and federal environmental usage laws? In most American cities, busy street corners historically had gas stations on them. Many of those gas stations closed down decades ago and abandoned storage tanks deep underground. Current owners of that property—even those who may be the fifth or sixth or even more remote owners—have current liability exposure from leaks coming out of those abandoned (and usually not completely empty) tanks.

Builders' codes and zoning. General contractors have the expertise to comply with building code rules in their cities. A good homebuilder will factor in the time and cost of pulling permits for everything from electrical and plumbing infrastructure to compliance with hurricane rules on roofing.

Zoning is a separate but related issue that comes up in building trades. Knowing the zoning ordinances can be an offensive move in addition to a defensive move. In my hometown, there are rules preventing bars from operating within one hundred yards of a "church door." My church installed a new door just about ninety yards from the property line of a local bar just in case we someday want to get them closed down!

Labor law and FMLA. Some readers may have sought protection under the Family Medical Leave Act when they applied for time off for health matters. You may also be generally aware of the Americans with Disabilities Act but don't really know how it might apply to accessibility or right to work and accommodations requirements in your new company.

Data privacy. Less obvious are rules that protect consumers' data. The area of data privacy protection is evolving very rapidly in the European Union and the United States. Any company gathering consumer data needs to understand how those privacy rules impact the gathering, storing, using, and reselling of consumer data.

In 2020 alone, I worked with my team of lawyers on several software exit transactions that ultimately collapsed because the sellers had failed to pay appropriate attention or dedicate the right resources to domestic and international privacy laws.

Professional licensing. You probably know that your doctor, veterinarian, hair stylist, manicurist, and lawyer all must have current state licenses to provide services in their chosen professions. But did you know that a home entertainment system installer or a florist needs a license in some states? Also, childcare and eldercare providers and electricians … there are dozens of occupations requiring professional licenses for the individuals and sometimes special licenses for the companies hiring those individuals.

You can and should do some basic industry research on your own at the very earliest phases of developing your business plan. Joining trade groups, staying on top of the latest legislative trends, and actively participating in online and in-person dialogues will give you some idea of what legal boundaries might exist in your business.

Some frequent hidden regulatory traps include the following:

- ADA
- Family Medical Leave Act
- data privacy rules (Europe, UK, and California are much more strict than everywhere else)
- environmental and hazardous material disposal
- zoning issues (make sure you understand these when you sign a lease)
- trademark and copyright rules (addressed in more detail in a later chapter)
- local trade union compliance (especially in government contract work)
- "Made in America" rules (especially in sales to the military)
- professional licensing rules (these apply to all kinds of professions that you wouldn't expect them to)

Don't trust your lawyer. I mean it. Not all lawyers know all laws. Data privacy, for example, is not my thing. Neither is environmental law or labor law. I would not presume to wing it in those areas even if my client asked me to do it. I am well supported by a team of experts in those fields who educate both me and my clients.

The practice of law is like the practice of medicine. Everyone needs a solid general practice business lawyer like they need a family doctor or internist to look out for their general well-being, but you probably would not ask your family doctor to put in a cardiac stent. And you shouldn't trust your general business lawyer to manage your compliance with specialized regulatory affairs.

Rocket Fuel Story. Poor Luke, he's still recovering from the required arbitration over the breach of contract when he receives a notice from the Department of Defense requesting him to fill out about one hundred forms detailing all his sales for the past six months. Someone has anonymously reported Rocket Fuel is selling fuel stock to North Korea. In fact, Rocket Fuel does have a contract for the sale of a small, sample shipment of fewer than fifty barrels to Vietnam. But

they do not have any knowledge of a contract with North Korea. Rocket Fuel hires a government contracting lawyer to help with the paperwork and reporting obligations. They work with a customs lawyer to find out if there has been a mix-up in the paperwork. And they end up having to cancel the sale to Vietnam based on an inability to prove that the fuel will be used in Vietnam and not reexported.

Compliance with government regulations increases the cost of overseas sales by more than 100 percent. Rocket Fuel decides to stop all foreign sales and regroup around domestic purchasers until they are large enough to justify the overhead.

Law Firm Story. Shayla comes back to the office after a networking lunch excited to announce a new client for the firm. They are a family office located in Houston but representing a family in Guatemala. The family office representative was impressed with Shayla's fluency and cultural understanding of Central American business practices and eager to find affordable business counsel to help them set up  new investment entities in the United States. They offered to pay a large $100,000 retainer upfront. This is the first foreign business client for the firm. They talk to the prospective clients' counsel in Guatemala and to their US accounting firm. The US accounting firm is a small, very private firm that works only with Latin American clients. The family office does not yet have any US bank accounts because they have not yet formed or funded any US companies.

Maggie recently watched the film *Laundromat* and was a bit nervous about the firm taking on a new client from outside of the US with so few connections to established US institutions. She went on the American Bar Association's website to do a bit of digging and found out that law firms, like banks, are supposed to avoid accidental participation in money-laundering schemes. Maggie asked Shayla to investigate the OFAC requirements before accepting the $100,000 retainer or getting an engagement letter. After a few weeks of digging (and a call to the chair of the local International Bar Association), Shayla learned the process for clearing new foreign clients. Jorge attended a Bar Association seminar on setting up internal checks, and they contacted their professional liability insurance carrier to have their process approved. After that, they were much more careful about screening new foreign-owned clients.

CHAPTER 10

Protecting Your Intellectual Property

The intellectual property (IP) tool kit includes different tools for protecting expression of ideas based upon the nature of the expression. The tools include patents, trade secrets, trademarks, copyrights, and agreements. Trademarks and copyrights have been discussed. Agreements also should be considered an important part of your IP tool kit, as agreements enable you to negotiate with someone else to get what you want or what you need for your company to prosper.

For example, I once witnessed a pitch to an angel group where the entrepreneur had invented a cloth that soaked up oil spills and could clean up the dirtiest garage with very little effort. All the angels in the room were quite impressed. However, when asked if he had any IP rights, the entrepreneur responded that he did not need any IP rights. The mood in the room changed, as the angels wanted to know how the entrepreneur could be so cavalier about the inability of others to copy his invention without the deterrent of some form of IP protection. The entrepreneur had the perfect answer. The product was made from a material that could only be obtained from two mines in the entire world. The entrepreneur had secured exclusive rights to the mined material for use in his cloth. No one else could obtain the key material without causing the mine operator to violate the exclusive rights agreement, which would be enforceable in court. The angels opened their wallets.

Thus, IP protection is not always necessary for a successful product. You may use agreements to protect yourself in many situations. However, some form of IP protection is necessary for a successful business, as IP protection is needed to allow for return on investment in development of new products and bringing them to market. Otherwise, the value of the product may be driven to the marginal cost of copying the product by someone else.

What's in a Name

You've noticed by now that some of our core story companies don't yet have names. It's actually more difficult than you might think to find a suitable name for a company. There are multiple legal, IP, and marketing factors that play into name selection.

Legal: Your official legal company name cannot be too similar to the names of other companies in the states where you plan to do business.

IP: Your name (and brand/logo) cannot infringe on someone else's protected name or mark.

Marketing: Your name needs to be suitable for promoting your business and telling your story.

Domain name: It may be expensive to obtain the domain name you want.

An experienced marketing professional should understand these issues at least at a high level. So, it may be worth it to pay for some marketing assistance as you develop your business plan.

Note that it can cost $500 or more to change your legal name and much more to fight over tradenames and trademarks, so pay attention to your name at the beginning of the game and choose wisely.

> **Law Firm Story**. Shayla, Jorge, and Maggie don't have a name for their law firm yet. They want to use something clever but need to understand both the trademark rules for their logo and also the local state bar rules that restrict what kinds of names a law firm can officially use. They settle on a traditional law firm name (after bickering about whose name comes first). Then they decide they want to get domain names and file for protection around "windlaw," "solarlaw," "ecolaw," and "greenlaw" just in case they want to use those in the future for marketing purposes.

It's pretty clear that you can't choose someone else's name for your new business. But how can you find out if the name is taken? And what does it hurt to try?

> **Camp Car Story**. Thelma and Louise decide that the right name for their RV park–focused short-term rental company should evoke adventures and convenience and reliability. The KOA or Kampgrounds of America name has been used for generations to brand private, family-oriented RV campgrounds. They propose to their marketing firm that they use the name KOA Kwik Car or KKC. Their clever logo design (whipped up by one of their smart college kids) has an image of an RV against a sunset with a tiny car in front. Since both "KOA" and "Kwik" evoke well-established brands, it seems like a winner. But their marketing group recommends that they hire a branding lawyer to clear it first. Sure enough, the branding lawyer smells lawsuits and injunctions all over the place with the proposed name and perhaps the logo too. It takes four months of back and forth before they find a name that can be protected, is fun for marketing, and makes everyone involved excited. Since they stalled out at the beginning on naming, though, they formed a company using the generic name "Camp Car Company" and later adopted DBAs and URLs using the official name.

But please don't practice law without a license or allow your accountant or best friend or investor who has closed four prior deals to do so. It will cost you money in the long run.

Trademarks

Trademark rights, unlike copyrights, do not arise from mere creation. In the US, trademarks are meaningless until they are associated, in the minds of relevant consumers, with the product bearing the trademark. They are an indicator of source. The policy rationale for trademark protection is that trademarks provide consumers a simple means of knowing what sort of quality to expect when they purchase a product. Everyone knows what to expect from a Mercedes sedan and a Domino's pizza.

But did they when the first Mercedes car was introduced? Famous brands become famous and become strong trademarks through years of consistent use on products of similar quality.

A trademark is a brand name. A trademark includes any word, name, symbol, device, or any combination used to identify and distinguish the goods or services of one seller or provider from those of others, and to indicate the source of those goods and services.

The challenge for you as a new business owner is to come up with a name for your company and your products (which need not be the same) that qualifies as a trademark but is not similar to someone else's trademark or business name for similar or possibly related goods and services.

There are two steps, which may need to be repeated several times until you find a mark that meets both criteria:

1. Select a mark that qualifies for trademark protection under federal trademark law. The stronger the mark, the easier it will be to protect it.
2. Select a mark that will not cause a likelihood of confusion with those of someone else. This phase of the process is called a clearance search.

Selecting a Strong Mark

Trademark law does not protect words that are generic for the goods and services, such as *juice* for a juice bar. Generic names are incapable of being indicators of sources. Words that are merely descriptive are also not protected, unless the owner can show it has "acquired distinctiveness." For example, *back office* for software for office administration is descriptive.

Trademark law protects marks that are suggestive, such as One A Day for vitamins. Suggestive marks suggest a feature or characteristic of the good without describing it. The strongest marks, and easiest to protect, are fanciful and arbitrary marks, because they are inherently distinctive and are immediately source identifiers. They are often creative—made-up words, such as Lululemon—or words that have no relation to the goods, such as Apple for computers.

It is sometimes difficult to find a mark that suggests your product without being descriptive. Marketing departments often come up with nontrademark names like Bofo Beef for hamburgers because they readily convey the type of product. It is harder to launch products with arbitrary names like Atari for computer games. Tesla is an excellent trademark because it suggests electricity, but it does not describe an electric car. A trademark lawyer can help you distinguish (no pun) between a descriptive and a suggestive mark.

Clearance Search

Your mark is likely to cause confusion with another company's trademark if it is similar in sight, sound, or meaning and your goods are similar or related. The US Patent and Trademark Office will not register your mark if it finds a likelihood of confusion with a prior registered mark. More importantly, a prior user will sue you if you go to market with a product under a mark similar to theirs, on similar goods.

A clearance search includes a review of all registered marks in the US (or worldwide, if you are not limiting your market to the US), marks that are not registered (common law marks), domain names, and trade names. The scope, as to products, includes your product, as well as related products and services, and those that could reasonably be expected to be from the same source. For example, Thelma and Louise are renting campers. Their trademark clearance search would include campers, cars, trucks, vacation rental services, tents, and motels. And maybe sleeping bags.

The worst-case scenario is to spend five years building a business and reputation under a particular mark, only to have someone come out of the woodwork, asserting trademark infringement right before your next big funding round. And yes, that happened to one of my clients. Prior counsel never ran a full search, perhaps because the client did not want to pay for it. Spend the $1,500!

You may worry that all of the words in the English language have already been used as trademarks. That would be OK, because trademark rights only extend to the particular goods and services sold under those marks and a reasonable penumbra around them. For example, Ford is a registered trademark for a modeling agency and for cars. This leads us to the unique (not another pun) problem with domain names: who gets to use the ford.com domain name?

Trademarks versus Domain Names

The fact that a domain name is available says nothing about whether someone owns that name as a trademark for one or more products. More importantly, there is no IP right to a domain name independent of trademark rights. The ".com" is meaningless. Domain names are the result of a contract—the registration of the name with a domain name registrar by a business or individual (the registrant). The registration is time limited and expires if not renewed.

Trademarks are limited in geographic scope; domain names are not. When the internet was first commercialized, which trademark owner got to register the domain name was a huge problem. I worked on a dispute over the scrabble.com domain name. Ownership of the Scrabble trademark for the word game is not the same worldwide. The case settled with an agreement to share the landing page and direct US and Canadian visitors to the Hasbro Scrabble website and all other visitors to the Mattel subsidiary Scrabble site. http://www.scrabble.com/

Alicia and Michelle and Camp Car Company

Homework: Thelma and Louise need to select a brand name that is protectable as a trademark. Camp Car is generic. What names can you come up with that are suggestive or, better yet, arbitrary or fanciful? How would you categorize these names?
Fancy Nancy
Cassiopeia
Prairie Schooner
Conestoga
Whoa Nelly
Sapphire
Zogus

Copyrights

Copyrights are the rights creators have in their works that express an idea, embodied in a replicable medium, with at least a modicum of originality and creativity. Again, no one has any rights in ideas standing alone! And copyright law does not care how hard you worked.

Familiar examples of works entitled to copyright protection:

- music recorded on an iPhone
- lyrics written down
- the recording of the lyrics sung to the music
- the choreography of the modern dance written to be performed with the music
- the movie *West Side Story*

No copyrights:

- a speech that was given to a million people, but no one wrote it down or recorded it
- the song you made up for your toddler but did not write down or record
- the idea for a movie about a parent and a kid switching bodies
- a massive directory of phone numbers and addresses that took one thousand hours to compile
- the idea for a commercial for tacos featuring a talking Chihuahua

This section outlines what is important for new business owners to know as potential copyright owners and to avoid copyright infringement.

The most important thing to remember, aside from the fact that ideas are not protectable, is that copyrights belong to the creator of the work, unless the creator has already entered into a work-for-hire arrangement or is creating the work as part of her job. The copyrights come into existence the moment the creator "fixes" her original expression in a tangible medium.

For works created after January 1, 1978, copyrights live for the life of the creator plus seventy years, unless the work is a work-for-hire, in which case the term is ninety-five years from first publication or 120 years from creation, whichever expires first. The copyright for *The Great Gatsby* expires in 2020. This means that writers are now free to write stories based on the book.

Only certain kinds of work are protected by copyright:

- literary works, including computer program source code
- musical works
- dramatic works
- pantomimes and choreographic works
- pictorial, graphic, and sculptural works
- motion pictures and other audiovisual works
- sound recordings
- architectural works

There are no copyrights in ideas, procedures, processes, systems, methods, concepts, or discoveries.

There are five copyrights, usually thought of as a bundle of sticks. They are often transferred together but can be sold or licensed separately. These are the rights to:

- make copies
- make derivative works
- distribute copies to the public by sale, license, or other means
- perform the work publicly (this applies only to literary, musical, dramatic, choreographic, movies, and other audiovisual work and sound recordings)
- display the work publicly (this applies to the same works as above, plus pictorial, graphic, and sculptural works)

As a new business owner, you need to make sure that everyone who works for you understands that the creative work they do belongs to the business, either because they are employees or because you have signed a work-for-hire agreement with them before they start to work on the project.

You also need to be aware of other people's copyrights in the materials that you are using to create your business. You probably know that you need enterprise software licenses rather than personal software licenses for your business, you can't grab pictures from the internet to use on your websites, and you can't blast music at your corporate event without a license.

But you should also take a look at the materials you are relying on as the basis for any new materials. If they have copyrights, you are infringing when you create updated or improved materials. This is the definition of a derivative work. You cannot create derivative works without a license.

Know that you do not need to register your copyright with the US Copyright Office or use the © symbol to enforce your rights. If you do register and/or use the symbol, you will have a stronger case. The flip side is that the absence of the © on a photo or graphic is not a defense to using the image without permission. Savvy businesses hire copyright or advertising lawyers to review their materials before publication to make sure that the business is not inadvertently infringing anyone's copyrights.

You should also know that many software licenses prohibit the creation of derivative works. If you need to develop software to run your business, you are likely to find it much less expensive to use software licensed on an open-source basis. This does not mean that the owners do not have or assert copyrights. There are different flavors of open-source licenses. Many allow you to use the software commercially "for free," and to create derivative works, provided that you share back to the community your developments.

If the developed software is going to contribute to your competitive advantage, you are a fool to use open-source software without having a copyright lawyer review the licenses first. I once had a client who hired a software developer for their online reference website and failed to make the software work-for-hire or document the software before and after the developer worked on it. This is also a foolish mistake.

Rocket Fuel Story. Luke, Anakin, and Sally are fortunate to have been trained by Rice University and NASA. To test their engineered solutions, they need to run computer simulations. They need specialized software for this and have to write some of the code themselves. But they don't have the time or interest in writing an entire program from scratch. They use a program used by other Rice labs they have

worked in and modify and add to it as they create new simulations. They have no idea about the source of the original program, the scope of the license, or whether anyone is paying for it. They prepare a presentation for a conference in Switzerland to show off their cutting-edge advances. The third slide shows data from their simulations. Another attendee asks what software they are using to run the simulations. Luke answers honestly and moves on. Unfortunately, that attendee works for the owner of software and after the conference goes back to his San Jose office to confirm that Luke, Anakin, and Sally's lab has a license to use and modify the software. He discovers that the university's license expired five years ago and did not include a license for commercial use.

Rules of the Road

What do you do before downloading software to use in your business? Read the license! Even better, ask a copyright lawyer to read the license.

What if a colleague provides you with access to a software program? Ask her to show you the license.

Is it ever OK to use free software for a commercial purpose? Read the license! There are usually restrictions. Whether those restrictions matter to you depends on your particular situation.

Diamond Production Story. The founders all love *The Godfather*. They watch it together every chance they get. It is only natural that they decide it would be awesome to produce a new, feminist version called *The Godmother*. Cher agrees to play the lead. Elena Ferrante agrees to write the script. What better tribute to the original and to Martin Scorsese and Mario Puzo! Will Martin Scorsese and Mario Puzo be thrilled to see thew new *Godmother* at Sundance? Why not? What should Diamond Productions do to prevent litigation? The answer starts with L and ends with E.

What's in an Idea

So, you have a great idea! Congratulations! You are going to change the world! However, you are paranoid that someone is going to steal your idea and leave you with nothing. You are inclined to keep your idea a secret, but then you realize that no one will give you money or help you without understanding what you have in mind.

You decide to protect your idea from being stolen. You contact an IP lawyer to help you to protect your idea. You are shocked and dismayed to learn that an idea cannot be protected. Yes, that is correct, you cannot protect an idea! Only the expression of the idea can be protected. No one told you that! How do you protect the expression of an idea? That depends on the idea and the nature of the expression.

The rest of this chapter will focus on patents and trade secrets. In the case of patents and trade secrets, it is assumed that the "expression" of the idea is in the form of a technical advancement of some kind or a recognition or understanding of the physical world that, at least to your knowledge, has not been recognized by others. Patents allow inventors to use a limited monopoly position to protect the technical expression of their ideas to extract a price that more closely approaches the value that users receive from their inventions. Trade secrets can do the same but with the important requirement that the innovation must be of a nature that can be kept secret and that significant steps are taken to maintain the secret. Patent rights are secured by statute, with many formal requirements. For example, to secure patent rights, you must disclose your invention to the public. Once obtained, patent rights are generally the most protective and can last up to twenty years. Trade secret protection can be equally valuable but only applies if the secret is maintained, which does not happen automatically. You must take significant steps to keep your innovation a secret, and the innovation must be of the type that is not easily discoverable through reverse engineering or other analysis (like the formula to Coca-Cola).

In other cases, other barriers to competition may be sufficient (e.g., specialized knowledge). In the case of specialized knowledge, the key is to protect the specialized knowledge by locking up the person or persons with the specialized knowledge. Once again, contracts become important!

Patents

So, if patents are not required, when would a patent be appropriate? A patent is a competitive tool that confers the following advantages:

1. Right to prohibit copying for a period of time
2. Improve bargaining position/trading with competitors
3. Improve corporate image
4. Provide an entree to new markets
5. Provide royalties/profit center
6. Enable legal action for infringement, even if infringement is innocent
7. Reverse engineering is not a defense
8. Provide collateral for investments

What do you need to do to secure a patent? You start by providing a description of your invention. You may also search for "prior art"—that is, examples of the closest existing technology implemented previously by you or by others. If satisfied that your innovation is significantly different from (not anticipated by or "obvious" over) the prior art, you are ready to start the patenting process. Now you are ready to call your patent attorney.

Your patent attorney will ask you if you wish to file a provisional or a nonprovisional patent application, which really boils down to timing and cost considerations. The provisional application is a placeholder application that is not examined but enables you to defer the beginning of the twenty-year patent term for a regular, nonprovisional patent application by up to one year. A provisional application does not require claims but does require a written description of the invention that satisfies the disclosure requirements of the patent statute (i.e., another person skilled in the art could reproduce the invention from your description). To be effective, the description in the provisional application must expressly support claims made in the nonprovisional application describing the scope and content of your invention.

A provisional application may be filed in one or more of the following situations:

1. The innovator is short on funds and expects that to improve significantly within the next year.
2. The innovator is about to make a commercial presentation or present a paper.
3. Research is ongoing, and the invention will be supplemented numerous times in the near future.
4. Commercial prospects are unclear.
5. Corroboration of inventive activities is desired by filing with the government.
6. Secure proof of inventive activities prior to a relationship with another party.
7. Establish an early filing date to predate the inventive activities of others.
8. Add a year to your patent life.

To secure patent protection, you will need to prepare (typically using a patent attorney or patent agent) an application for your innovation that meets all the requirements for patentability:

1. New
2. Useful
3. Nonobvious, and
4. Provides an enabling written description of the innovation to one skilled in the art

The parts of a patent include drawings, a title, a field of the invention, a summary of the invention, a brief description of the drawings, a detailed description of the invention, examples, and claims defining the novel features of the invention. The scope of the patent claims should be broad enough to describe the novel features of the "special sauce" of the product and, ideally, should also be broad enough to cover a competitor's product as well as other products and markets in which the innovation could be applied (assuming the known "prior art" permits such as scope). It is important to keep in mind that a patent application must be filed within one year of a public use, a disclosure in a printed publication, an offer for sale, or a sale of your invention. International patent rights may be lost if a patent application is not filed before the public use or disclosure or transfer to another party.

So, how many patents are needed? Sometimes, as with software development, the head start advantage by being first to market with a new invention may be enough incentive to promote research investment, suggesting lighter IP protections needed. On the other hand, high-risk products, like pharmaceuticals, have high risk reward and longtime horizons that suggest stronger IP protections are needed. Thus, it is important to balance risk and reward to determine the proper amount of patent protection.

If the innovation was not publicly used or disclosed or transferred to another party before the US provisional or nonprovisional patent application was filed, then international patent rights may be secured so long as the international patent applications are filed within one year of the earliest US patent application filing. The Patent Cooperation Treaty (PCT) provides a mechanism for one patent application to be filed that is searched and examined prior to entry in any of a number of foreign jurisdictions that are part of the PCT. The international examination process provides the opportunity to identify prior art that may limit or prevent patent protection in other countries before undergoing the significant costs of translations, filing fees, and so on.

An important part of deciding whether to seek a patent is determining whether you have the *secret sauce.*

Identifying the "special sauce" to patent is not always easy. The special sauce could be:

1. Efficiencies in manner of production
2. Efficiencies in purchasing and using materials
3. Efficiencies in operating equipment
4. Efficiencies in managing accounting practices
5. Improvements by saving manufacturing costs

Once the special sauce has been identified, the key for patent protection is to secure one or more patents that prevent others from using the special sauce in a meaningful way. Think strategically. I like to use the Strait of Hormuz analogy (see the map to remind you of this strategic geographic juggernaut). If your task is to protect the flow of oil out of the Persian Gulf, what would be the most effective and efficient way to do so? I recommend placing an aircraft carrier in the Strait of Hormuz. When evaluating your product, what feature or combination of features is/are required to compete with you effectively? Use the Strait of Hormuz approach to secure patents that make it difficult to design around such features by placing patents in strategic locations around the features.

There are many nuances to securing meaningful patent protection. We do not recommend that you try it on your own. It takes many years to not only learn the nuanced patent laws but also to learn the technology to a degree that not only enables securing of patents in the Patent Office but also enables successful enforcement in the courts.

Do your homework to determine what can be patented and what should be patented in a cost-effective and timely way.

Rocket Fuel Story. Luke, Anakin, and Sally's rocket fuel is a combination of constituents that Luke, Anakin, and Sally analyzed during their research project. Luke, Anakin, and Sally discovered through their research efforts the exact combinations of constituents that would lead to the longest and most efficient burn that would save up to 25 percent on rocket fuel costs. Most of the constituents are commonly used; others have not been previously used in rocket fuels. The constituents may be determined by testing the fuel; however, the exact combination (percentage of each component) cannot be determined by testing.

Rice University is pushing hard to file as many patent applications as possible, as it would like to receive significant patent royalties to fund its chemical engineering department and to attract and retain top professors. Luke, Anakin, and Sally also would like to maximize the value of their company for sale in three to five years.

What aspects of the rocket fuel research project should Luke, Anakin, and Sally protect by patent? What aspects of the project, if any, should Luke, Anakin, and Sally protect by trade secret? What considerations went into your decision?

Trade Secrets

So, when should an innovation be kept as a trade secret? The innovation, by its nature, must be something that can be kept secret. Also, when a patent is difficult to enforce because infringement is difficult to discover and prove, trade secret protection may be the best alternative. For example, if you cannot determine if someone is copying your innovation without accessing a competitor's assembly line, then proving patent infringement may be an uphill challenge. However, it may be quite difficult to persuade someone to invest in an idea without disclosing it. Once the expression of your idea has been disclosed, you may have nothing left to sell. Unfortunately, the decision to disclose or not must be made early on since patent rights may be lost after exploitation of an invention.

Whether to protect by patent or trade secret requires you to ask yourself a few questions. For example:

- Is my innovation something that can be kept secret?
- If others have my product, can they reverse engineer the product and figure out my innovation?
- Is my innovation something that I can limit access to, like server software that is locked down in a server that is accessible only with a passcode?
- Is my product innovation something that will have a short shelf life, or is it something that will take many years to bring to market?

On the other hand, if you have determined that you can protect your innovation by keeping it a secret, what steps must you take? First, keep in mind that a trade secret is information used in a business, unknown to others, that provides a competitive advantage. Trade secrets are protected under common law, state civil statutes, and federal and state criminal statutes. Trade secret rights may last indefinitely if the secrecy can be maintained. Accordingly, the key to trade secrets protection is to put processes in place to identify and maintain trade secrets. The costs for such processes are not insignificant, and vigilance is required.

Set up an internal process to protect your trade secrets based on the answers to your homework. Follow these ten steps to secure trade secret protection in an annual audit:

1. Identify valuable trade secrets.
2. Develop a trade secret protection policy and put it in writing.
3. Educate employees about the policy and monitor compliance (e.g., use preemployment and exit interviews and have employees acknowledge continuing secrecy obligations when leaving).
4. Restrict trade secret access to a need-to-know basis.
5. Mark trade secret documents as such.
6. Physically isolate and protect the most important trade secrets.
7. Maintain secrecy of computers and computer files.
8. Restrict public access to facilities.
9. Use confidentiality agreements with third parties.
10. Have a policy for unsolicited submissions to your company.

CHAPTER 11

Buy-Sell Agreements

Buy-sell agreements are used for four types of events:

1. Settling disputes
2. Addressing the big Ds of death, divorce, disability, and disappearance
3. Redeeming an interest in a for-cause event
4. Granting protective rights in an exit event

It is impossible to discuss buy-sell agreements without also discussing *valuation*.

At the core of the first three is the uncertainty of determining value of the equity for the buyer or seller.

In the fourth, the market (usually an outside buyer) has set the value of the equity through an arms-length negotiation or auction process.

First—Settling Disputes

In Chapter 1, you learned that a fifty/fifty style of Leadership can and often does lead to deadlock. I recommended staying away from fifty/fifty deadlocks as frequently as possible by including an advisory council or other tiebreaking processes in your governance provisions. But sometimes, everyone just gets stuck. It is OK to walk away and agree to disagree in a business dispute—but each side needs to feel that they received fair value for their interests. One way to do that is to put a mandatory buy-out clause in the company agreement or buy-sell agreement.

The value of an interest is the tricky factor in fifty/fifty tiebreaking situations. One tool in the toolbox is the shotgun, a colorful Wild West image for a very elegant economic solution.

In a *shotgun sale*, Alligator and Crocodile are fifty/fifty partners and cannot get past the giant teeth. After working a bit with their advisory council and failing, Alligator makes an offer to buy out Crocodile at an agreed price (fixed or formulaic). Crocodile has x number of days to decide whether to accept the offer made by Alligator or to instead buy out Alligator on the same terms (or equivalent terms if their percentages are different). This is fair because both sides can come to their own conclusions about whether they prefer to buy or sell based on their own perception of the company's value.

Enron Unwind Story. I was assistant general counsel for Enron both before and after its bankruptcy. One of my jobs before bankruptcy was to put together gigantic joint ventures for the development of billion-dollar wind energy farms. After bankruptcy, I got to help take those apart. The unwind of these deals was relatively easy even though there were billions of dollars of assets involved, because each joint venture agreement included detailed buy-sell provisions addressing many possible scenarios.

Another way to do it is to *break the doughnut*—you know, like Mom telling the two kids to share the doughnut. One breaks it, and one picks her half. In this case, the owners want to divide up the assets and take their fair share in a division or liquidation of the company. One owner "breaks," and the other "chooses." This can be very simple but also works for billion-dollar complex portfolios.

Break the Doughnut Story. A major international energy company formed dozens of joint ventures for the operation of retail gas stations. Each joint venture owned several hundred stations. The tiebreaking/deadlock mechanism we built into those deals was basically a doomsday doughnut deal. If the operator of a pool of stations and the brand/supplier partner had irreconcilable differences, one of the parties had the right to divide the pool of stations into two presumably equally valuable groups. Then the other party had the first choice of picking one of the groups. This was simple, elegant, and very, very scary to both parties because it threatened to destroy the value created by having a single, intact group of locations. In fact, it was so scary to contemplate an ultimate meltdown resulting in a break-the-doughnut dissolution that everyone got along quite nicely for many, many years.

Mandatory buyouts can be helpful in management disputes as well as in tiebreaker situations. The value of an interest (discussed below) may be set in advance by the parties so that there is a peaceful way to remove an executive owner who is not a good fit.

Camp Car Story. Alicia and Michelle have a fifty/fifty venture. They know this is an unstable way to operate, but they believe with the effort they put into the Decision Matrix, the inclusion of Charlie as an adviser, and other checks and balances, they can make it work. Nevertheless, they decide that if there is a dispute so profound that they cannot proceed as partners, they are willing to submit to a tiebreaking buy-sell clause. Both the shotgun and the break-the- doughnut tools are suitable for a fifty/ fifty venture that will own multiple equivalent locations. But in their case, they decide that the value of the company is dependent upon having economies of scale. So, they build in a shotgun clause. Before exercising the shotgun, they are required to submit the dispute in good faith to Charlie and also to legal mediation. If those processes fail to repair their relationship, then either Alicia or Michelle can make an offer to buy or sell her share of the company at a stated price. The other partner has a choice.

Do I buy or do I sell? If she thinks the price is low, she will buy. If she thinks the price is high, she will sell.

Rocket Fuel Story. Luke, Marco, and Sally are all about the same age with similar educational and financial situations. Marco is engaged. They anticipate that their company quickly will grow much bigger than the three of them can or should manage. They consider the shotgun tool but decide that none of them will have the personal resources to buy out the others and that with outside investors, this tool could cause additional tension and uncertainty that could impair value.

They decide that in the event of irreconcilable differences in management styles or direction, they will allow the outsider to retire and be bought out by the company (not just the other founders) with a five-year note and an earn-out that can appreciate if the company has a significant exit or capital event while the note is in place. This is a compromise. But it will prevent the company from stalemate or losing value while they try to deal with personalities or changed life goals over time.

Of course, you need a good lawyer to craft any of these sophisticated buy-sell options.

Second—The Big Ds: Death, Disability, Divorce, Disappearance (Retire/Resign), Disaster (Personal)

In a large company where shares are widely held or in an investment fund with passive investors, the big Ds don't generally apply to passive owners and their families. A company is normally agnostic about the identity of the owner (exceptions exist) if all the company took was money. But big Ds really can hurt a company when they hit a key employee or a significant owner who is also involved in decision-making. They also matter tremendously in services companies.

Death and *disability* are fairly self-explanatory. In a company where there are key people holding equity, the company needs a way not only to replace the key person but also to buy out his or her interest. Insurance policies can play a big role in this process, both in settling up value and in funding the buyout. But often a company doesn't carry insurance or doesn't carry sufficient insurance to fund a redemption, and the company (or its other owners) need to make payments to the estate over time with a note. Value of the interest is a key concept—and it is far better to struggle with that before a big D event than after.

Divorce is a bit easier. Normally the parties will require a divorcing owner to buy out the spousal interest anytime there is a community property event, including death or divorce of the spouse. Set the value of the interest in the agreement; it is much safer than arguing over it in divorce court.

Disappearance, well, that's a strange one. But believe it or not, it happens with alarming regularity in start-up companies. I once had a missing founder who owned 8 percent of a biotech company and had grown weary of life. He just walked off the planet, leaving little trace. We managed to get the company sold without him, and I heard that he had bought a shack in Indonesia or something.

Disappearance also refers to both retirement and general change of personal direction. Sometimes a founder needs a change—needs a way out. His wife got the dream job in Houston, and they need to move. He decided his life's passion was being an Iron Man, not the founder of a start-up (same grit required, different muscles). Maybe the founder jumped in when he was sixty and thought it would only take five years—and now it is year seven. Companies with key people owning equity need a way to peacefully deal with the disappearing members.

Note that sometimes companies, especially service companies, come up with different buyout rights for long-tenured employee owners who are actually retiring versus active employee owners who decide to jump ship for a better opportunity. The role of noncompete, nonsolicitation, and similar restrictive covenants is beyond the scope of this discussion, but it can influence the value payable to different kinds of disappearing employee owners.

Disaster comes out of nowhere, or at least appears to come out of nowhere. This is the catch-all phrase to address the personal bankruptcy, bad behavior, or other inconvenient disabling conduct that prevents an individual or corporate owner from continuing to own equity without creating complications. Normally, buy-sell agreements treat these disaster events as nonevents for passive investors (unless someone is truly making headlines for their bad behavior). But if a founder or significant owner/employee owner is involved, the buy-sell terms should lay out the path for the company to redeem the equity of the disaster owner. Note that if the disaster is truly bad behavior, such as fraud, malfeasance, personal activities that impact the company's reputation, or criminal activities, the buy-sell usually provides for a quick buyout for a significantly discounted price.

Law Firm Story. Imagine Shayla, Maggie, and Jorge as fit and fabulous sixty-year-olds. They have built a strong regional law firm with twenty partners and sixty other staff attorneys and paraprofessionals. Maggie has become increasingly involved in a national charity and is taking on regional and possibly national leadership roles as her thousands of volunteer hours pay off. She can imagine herself continuing to practice law for ten to twenty hours each month on cases important to her. But the daily commitment to running the firm and actively carrying a full-time load is not there. The partners worked with their advisers in 2018 (after Shayla had a health scare) to talk about succession plans for leadership and fair buy-sell terms. They have a committee of leaders now that includes some of the younger partners. And they agreed to a buyout formula for when a partner wants to retire. Maggie agrees to retire on the terms set out in the buy-sell in exchange for a payout over time. Then she stays with the law firm as a part-time employee, taking the title "partner emeritus." Jorge has twelve grandchildren and a lake house. He thinks that Maggie's deal might be just the right thing for him in two years.

For Cause—The Ultimate Headache

It happens. Anakin gets angry one too many times and turns his light saber on the wrong people. Harvey Weinstein, well, you know. Really horrible things can happen because, after all, we are dealing with humans. Hollywood makes a fortune off the age-old story of good guys gone wrong (*Ozark*, *Breaking Bad*). Wall Street produces heroes and villains of its own each day.

When someone goes rogue, the company needs a way to remove the bad apple. Don't sign an agreement or enter a room without an exit sign for emergencies. Plan for the worst and work for the best. And be prepared for a lawsuit even if you have a very well drafted agreement.

Thinking Ahead to an Exit

In private companies that intend to exit in a sale to a larger company or perhaps even go public, there are three additional buy-sell clauses you need to understand:

1. The tagalong
2. The drag-along
3. Registration rights

The first two are very common and easy to understand.

A tagalong clause prevents the majority owners from selling out from under the minority owners without giving the minority owners a fair share of the exit proceeds. It evokes the image of a younger sibling tagging along with his or her big sister to the fun event (the sale).

Drag-along prevents the minority owners from standing in the way of a lucrative exit that the majority wants to accept. It evokes the same familiar imagery of a parent dragging a child along to an event that is more important to the parent than the child.

Registration rights are very technical clauses setting out the rules of the road for all owners in case of a public offering. They are complicated and have elements of tagalong and drag-along clauses as well as detailed holding period rules and references to securities laws. Many form documents still have these clauses in them from the dot-com boom when every new company hoped and dreamed of going public quickly. Going public is rarely the first exit option or even the second for companies formed today. So, including these difficult-to-read and long clauses in buy-sell agreements is usually unnecessary in the first phase of the company's life.

Valuing an Equity Interest

In Chapter 1, we talked about company value in the context of selling equity to raise capital. Company value is also a key element in buy-sell agreements, but it is only part of the puzzle. Ultimately, in a buy-sell event, you need to know the value of the equity interest to be sold, not just the company value.

The value of an equity interest can be a more difficult topic. Often parties will fix the value of an equity interest in advance through contractual agreement or by agreeing to a formula to use when calculating the value of an equity interest.

Example: The parties agree that if the company removes a member for cause, the value of the equity interest owned by the removed member is $100.00.

In this example, the value of the equity interest is a punitive value set very low as a form of damages for the bad behavior resulting in the removal for cause.

Example: The parties agree that upon the divorce of a member, the community property interest owned by the nonmember spouse is valued at half the positive capital account balance of the divorcing member.

In this example, the value of the equity interest is not negotiable at the time of sale and could be quite low depending on the capital account balance.

Example: The parties agree that the value of the equity interest of a key employee owner exercising his or her put right is equal to the sharing ratio of the owner multiplied by the company value. They stipulate that the company value is the sum of the fair market values of the portfolio assets held by the company.

In this example, the company holds readily valued assets like publicly traded stock, investment real estate, or similar passive investments. The value of the company is deemed to be the sum of its parts. And the value of the owner's equity interest is his or her percentage ownership multiplied by the company value.

But these are the easy cases. It gets more difficult when the company is an operating company or a company in the early stages or holding diverse and difficult to value assets. It is also difficult to find the value of an interest in a services company like a law firm or accounting firm.

One solution is to appoint an appraiser or to create a process for appointing an appraiser who can assist in determining both the company value and the value of the equity.

Another is to create a formula as a backstop value for the company value; this works in industries (such as insurance companies) where there are accepted multiples of earnings-based valuations across the market.

Sometimes a formula serves as a placeholder and is disregarded in the event of a sale or capital raise that closes during a designated window after the buy-sell event.

There are dozens of other solutions that work in different circumstances, including blind bid processes, auctions, and formulas. And there are experts in buy-sell valuations and processes for hire at many price points.

Important Fact

The company value is almost always greater than the sum of the value of the equity interests. What do we mean? An owner of a 20 percent, nonvoting, common interest subject to restrictions on transferability has much less power over the company than the owner of a majority interest entitled to a preferred return who has the right to sell her interest. For estate planning, tax planning, and other purposes, it is sometimes very important to understand the discounted value of a minority or otherwise restricted interest. But in an exit, everyone wants his or her equity to be valued the same way as everyone else's equity of the same class. Buy-sell agreements need to carefully and clearly spell out that the valuation of the company and/or of any particular interest under the buy-sell agreement is *irrelevant* in determining the fair market value of the company for other commercial purposes.

> **Important Note**. This book focuses on building a strong team of founders, investors, and advisers. Crafting buy-sell agreements that are fair and realistic often requires parties to think about their family goals, personal financial situation, and their own health. Founders who seem equal on the surface may, in fact, have very different risk factors and risk tolerances in the context of health issues, succession discussions, and the role of family in carrying on original company goals. Different founders may

have very different economic needs and access to capital. Each founder needs its own team of advisers (not the company's corporate lawyer) who can advise on the impact of proposed buy-sell provisions as the company's value increases.

A founders' family team should include a good accountant, an estate-planning lawyer, a financial adviser with strong experience in working with closely held businesses, and a creative life insurance adviser with solid tax knowledge. Advisers who regularly counsel private company owners have strong interdisciplinary networks. Ask your business lawyer or your personal financial adviser for introductions as the first step in building a cohesive team. These family-focused advisers can coordinate with one another using their skills to make sure your buy-sell agreement is not at cross-purposes with other long-term goals.

CONCLUSION

So now what happens? You have laid a solid foundation for your company using the tools in this book. Perhaps you have raised money and feel an obligation to make good on your promises to investors. Maybe that ninety-day plan stretched to 360 days or more, and you still need to find that breakthrough after meeting your first set of goals. It could be that you have a solid operating company generating good cash flow and meeting the expectations of founders and investors.

But nothing lasts for long. Change is inevitable and in fact healthy. This book will help you weather the storms of change and give you confidence to adapt in logical and well-planned ways.

Put a date on the calendar for eighteen months from now. Open this book again then. Flip through some of your original homework and see if it still makes sense.

Plan a reunion pizza meeting—perhaps with some new personalities and talents at the table. Do you need a reset on the management style? Maybe you have functioned as an enlightened dictatorship but are getting pressure from investors to evolve into a representative democracy? Maybe you have one or two new key players. Before you issue equity to the newcomers, have you really gotten to know them using the worksheets in Chapters 1 and 2?

Maybe you need to brush up on the basics of contracts now that you have a steadier flow of business and are starting to expand your activities.

Almost certainly, you could use a touch-up look at your buy-sell agreement (or maybe now is the time you can breathe long enough to put one in place). You might have a better idea of the long-term group dynamics and the valuation puzzle.

Most transactional lawyers will give you an annual checkup for free if you ask. Take the book and the homework in with you to that checkup to restart the conversations.

To help guide you through planning for the future, let's see how our core stories play out after a few years of operations.

No one's journey is easy. And not every story has a happy ending. But you can significantly increase your odds of seeing it through the rough times and building something that you are proud of if you take care of the Human Factor first. Put the right people in the right positions. Set goals. Understand your objectives in contractual relationships. Surround yourself with experienced advisers. Be flexible. Regroup. Buy more pizza. Plan for the future with good buy-sell agreements. And find your exit—in two years, ten years, or thirty years.

See if you can imagine your Human Factors in the future as you read the long-term conclusions to our original core stories.

Law Firm Story. You've already seen the law firm zip forward twenty years in the preceding chapter. The three original partners checked back in with the nuts and bolts of group dynamics every three or four years as their practice grew to include first younger associates and later equity partners. They remained flexible in changing their management style over time. For almost a decade, Shayla was the  de facto enlightened dictator, making major decisions for the group and providing strong but kind leadership. She enjoyed it and was respected by the others. In fact, Jorge and Maggie really didn't like the back-office work anyway. But over time, Shayla needed help. First, they needed to upgrade their technology platform and way of working remotely, and one of the senior associates became very involved in that project. Then they added new practice areas and looked to two new partners to lead. Risk management and shopping for insurance required annual dedication. And the financial side of the business became more complicated.

First, Shayla formed ad hoc committees. Then the partners voted to create a board. Over time, they shifted away from an enlightened dictatorship to a representative democracy that divided responsibilities among a group of six people. This became the long-term solution to leadership, allowing Maggie (and later Jorge and Shayla) to consider stepping back and eventually retiring.

They created jobs, culture, and a legacy through their law firm. As each of the founders retired, the firm endowed a scholarship for minority law students at their alma maters in the name of each founder to honor that legacy of leadership and commitment to diversity.

Rocket Fuel Story. In their initial pizza meetings, Luke, Marco, and Sally set the goal of selling the company in five years. You may remember that unlike many businesses, they started out with serious and seasoned investors and allies from Rice University and the Houston angel community. They built an advisory board of mentors  from the industry that included some very impressive and ambitious leaders in the private rocket-launching community. Marco moved out of the US to his home country. But he maintained an active and engaged leadership role from afar and traveled regularly back to Houston to meet with the team and investors.

There were some hurdles to overcome. They tried to expand too quickly outside of the US market and ran into regulatory and export restrictions. They needed more equity and sold approximately 20 percent to a venture capital fund in year four.

They outsourced the manufacturing of the fuel (mostly a mixing of existing feed stock) to an experienced international chemical company in Houston. But they didn't have a backup plan. When the chemical company decided to restructure their internal priorities, they slowed down and eventually stopped production. A lawsuit, significant negative publicity over missed deadlines and deliveries, and some difficult discussions with investors followed, dragging the company down for more than two years.

Rice was assertive about its royalty rights. The profits from fuel sales were lower than they originally projected because of this override that the founders didn't really understand upfront.

But they overcame the obstacles. Texas became a solid center for private space companies, and demand increased. Offers for the purchase of the company started coming in around the seventh anniversary. In year eight, the board recommended engaging an investment banking firm to package the company for sale. Around the ninth anniversary, the company was sold. Luke stayed on as chief engineer. Sally stayed only for a transitional leadership period of six months. Marco retired.

It took longer and cost more money than anyone could have imagined. There were dark days of lawsuits and investigations. But they stuck with it and cashed out successfully.

Diamond Productions Story. Diamond Productions was always more free form than the other projects in our core stories. Each of the founders brought different experiences and different dreams to the table. Their combined expertise and fame enhanced the individual projects each pursued. Underneath the holding company umbrella of the original company, they formed three different focused production companies, led by each founder. They also launched a foundation as a separate legal entity to be funded from Diamond's profits and to leverage the Diamond brand into strong fundraising for the foundation.

Christine focused on positive, women-centric stories with strong voices from historically underrepresented groups. Several of the films that she produced premiered at major festivals, and all landed distribution agreements for domestic and foreign streaming through well-known platforms. Her films won a couple of Golden Globes and Oscar nominations.

Tomas became interested in telling the stories of indigenous people in Latin America, using student filmmakers to create a documentary series in English, Spanish, and several local languages. He worked closely with several magazines to help develop print, film, and podcast versions of these stories. And he partnered with nonprofits in the regions where he filmed to support literacy and preservation of local cultures.

Elara found that her true passions were acting and writing. She continued to work on film and television projects as an actress as her primary focus for many years. Writing pilots for large-scale, episodic films was just a hobby at first. But she found her voice writing about a group of teenage activists from the Trump years. Her pilot became a six-episode series. Then it was picked up by a major network for additional seasons. It became a popular platform for young political activists to make cameo appearances, and it inspired a new generation of social media–empowered changemakers. Elara and Christine collaborated on a feature film musical based on the characters from the series.

Much like the law firm, Diamond Productions nurtured the next generation of leadership and created a legacy company. The buy-sell agreement of the founders allowed each to keep no more than 10 percent of the company in their respective families after they stepped out of leadership. That made space for new leaders to earn equity ownership and make their mark over time.

Alicia and Michelle. Michelle was diagnosed with breast cancer. Alicia and Michelle negotiated a buyout that they both agreed was fair. About six months after Alicia bought out Michelle, their company was featured on a national business reality show after Michelle's son sent in an audition tape without anyone's permission. The publicity from the show was great. Two private equity groups with strong histories of successful investment in camping, mobile homes, and outdoor recreation knocked on the door with offers more than double what the founders expected when they executed the separation agreement to buy out Michelle's interest.

After working with Charlie and an investment banking group to consider the options, Alicia decided to sell 75 percent of the company, with an option to sell the remaining 25 percent in another three years. Michelle had retained 10 percent of the company in her exit. Also, the exit agreement with Michelle included the ability to reprice if there was a significant difference in price in an equity raise or exit within a year after her sale. Michelle opted to sell her remaining 10 percent under the tagalong clause, and the repricing rights yielded her an additional $1.5mm.

Alicia, one of her daughters, and one of Michelle's sons remained actively involved in the business after the sale. After recovering from breast cancer, Michelle built her dream home on Lake Tahoe and welcomed all of the now-adult children of the founders and their families for annual winter ski breaks and fun summer gatherings.

GLOSSARY

accredited investor. An investor who meets certain income or net worth minimum requirements either individually or as part of a household. The definition is applicable when determining how and from whom to raise funds in a private offering.

angel. This is a common term for an early-stage investor who brings money to the table, often before there is much more than a good idea. The best angels bring time, expertise, or connections as mentors along with their money. Angels often invest through angel networks that meet as breakfast clubs or other networking groups to host prospective companies making pitches.

asset sale. A sale of all or most of the assets of a company to a buyer.

at will. See *common contract clauses.*

B corporation. A type of corporation that elects to governed as a public benefit corporation under the laws of its state of formation.

bad behavior. Buy-sell agreements often define "for cause" events that result in a quick and heavily discounted buyout of a person who has engaged in behavior that the company agrees could be harmful to the economics, reputation, or leadership dynamics of the company. Examples include fraud, conviction of a felony, self-dealing, misusing company property, breaching key provisions of the agreements (like noncompetes, nondisclosures etc.), or engaging in the kind of activities that the company does not want to see in the newspaper. The definition is negotiable. And lists differ. In the era of #MeToo and heightened awareness of the value of diversity, inclusion, and respect for differences, lists of bad behavior are growing longer to include embarrassing behavior and not just illegal behavior.

big Ds. These are described in Chapter 11 and include some of the common triggering events under buy-sell agreements, such as death, divorce, disability, disappearance, and disaster.

board or **board of directors**. The group of individuals elected by the shareholders by following the rules in the bylaws. The board has supervisory control over the officers and plays a long-term and strategic role over the direction of the company. Shareholders can both elect and remove directors following the rules in the bylaws.

bylaws. The rule book adopted by corporations setting out the hierarchical relationship and voting rights between shareholders, the board of directors, and officers. These are formal rule books following both statutory law and hundreds of years of common practice.

buy-sell agreement. The contract defining the restrictions on owners in transferring their ownership interests and the rights of owners to participate in sales by other owners. In an LLC or partnership, the buy-sell agreement is usually negotiated as part of the company agreement or partnership agreement. With a corporation, it is a stand-alone document adopted separately.

C corporation. A corporation that is taxed as a separate entity under the rules set out in Subchapter C of the Internal Revenue Code. A corporation is a C corporation unless it elects to be taxed as an S corporation or something else.

C-suite. A shorthand term for the most senior officers who report directly to the board or the managers. It commonly includes the CEO or chief executive officer, the CFO or chief financial officer, the COO or chief operating officer, and other "Cs" as called out for leadership in a particular organization.

call. The right to require someone to sell and ownership interest.

Cap Table or **capitalization table**. The official record of ownership, ownership percentages (sometimes called sharing ratios), and initial capital contributions in an LLC and the official record of shareholders and shares in a corporation. In a corporation, it usually takes the form of a stock registry.

charter or **certificate of formation**. The "birth certificate" formally accepted by the state of formation of a corporation, LLC, or limited partnership. This document can be long or short, depending on how much detail is required by state law for a particular entity. For corporations, this document sets out the economic rights of the different classes of ownership. For LLCs and limited partnerships, it is usually a very simple document with just basic information about the company, like its name, address, original managers/general partner, and birthday.

company agreement or **operating agreement**. Refers to the contract adopted by the members and managers of a limited liability company setting out their rules for governance, funding, tax, buy-sell, and other important details. Since the LLC statutes of most states are very vague about the rights of members and managers, it is important to work with a lawyer to draft a good company agreement.

common equity. The original founders' equity in a company, plus any additional equity issued without preferred returns or special voting or economic rights. Common equity (either shares in a corporation or units in an LLC) gets paid after debt and after preferred equity. But it shares in the biggest upside growth in a successful company.

copyright. The legal protection of an original written work, song, or artistic work. Some copyrights are granted automatically, and others may only be obtained by filing for protection with the USPTO. Copyrighted material can be called out with the symbol ©. See Chapter 10.

corporation. The legal form of entity chartered under state law. It is the most common form of entity used by public companies. Its formal, statutorily mandated structure protects shareholders, defines the roles of directors, and provides many rules around governance that the founders must follow to maintain liability protection.

derivative work. See *copyrights*.

disabling conduct. Can be part of the list of big Ds that trigger buyout rights under a buy-sell agreement. This is another way to describe bad behavior or for-cause activities.

disregarded entity (DRE). An LLC owned by a single company or individual that elects to be disregarded or ignored for federal income tax purposes. These are common in holding company structures with multiple subsidiaries formed for risk management and business segregation purposes.

employee. Not an *independent contractor*. See test in homework to evaluate the differences.

equity. A fractional ownership interest in a company. For corporations, these are shares. For LLCs and partnerships, these can be described as units or as membership interests or partnership interests.

equity sale. A sale of the equity of a company to a new owner. Usually refers to a sale of all or most of the equity outstanding to a new owner.

exempt offering. The sale of securities (or certain debt) in a private offering that qualifies for an exemption under the federal and state securities laws.

FOB. "Freight on board" is a common shorthand provision in contracts for the sale of goods. It specifies that the price includes the cost of delivery up to a specified location. Technically, your personal orders from Amazon are FOB your front door.

for cause. See *common contract clauses*. Often a synonym with disabling conduct or bad behavior in the context of buy-sell agreements.

force majeure. See *common contract clauses*.

foundation. See *nonprofits*.

founder. The individual or very small group of people who turn a good idea into an actual business.

fund. Typically refers to a group of investors who have pooled their money into an investment company that picks several target investments to support. A private equity fund can refer to individuals or family offices who pool their funds to identify target investments of a specific industry, such as an energy PE fund or a biotech PE fund. A venture capital fund is similar but often involves larger investments from institutional as well as private investors.

general partner. The partner in a general partnership with full-liability risk exposure and management responsibility.

general partnership. General partnerships can be formed informally with a handshake or written contract and are dangerously easy to form accidentally by agreeing to share profits and losses.

indemnity. See *common contract clauses.*

limited partners. The passive investor owners in a limited partnership. Their rights are defined by the partnership agreement. They cannot engage in any decisions or management activities in the ordinary course of the partnership's business, or they risk losing their limited liability status.

limited partnership. Limited partnerships must be formed with a charter or certificate of formation like corporations and LLCs. Limited partnerships must have a general partner who has full liability exposure to the debts of the entity. Limited partners are passive investors and, as long as they remain truly passive, generally have similar liability protection as shareholders in a corporation or members of an LLC.

limited partnership agreement. The partnership version of a company agreement.

LLC. Limited liability company is a common legal form of entity chartered under state law. Its owners obtain liability protection as investors. It is a more flexible form of entity than a corporation or a limited partnership because it can adopt its own style of governance by writing a company agreement or operating agreement that sets out the rules on how owners and management interact and what their expectations are in economic, governance, tax, and other areas. Normally, LLCs elect to be taxed as partnerships. This is the most common form of entity for early stage and for private companies at any stage of operation.

manager. LLCs often elect to be managed by managers. The manager can be a single leader, operating like the CEO, or can be part of a board, functioning like a corporate board of directors. The rules setting out the role of the manager are in the company agreement and vary significantly from company to company.

member. Usually, the owners of LLCs are referred to as members, not as shareholders. Their rights are defined by the company agreement / operating agreement of the LLC.

membership interest. A fraction of ownership in an LLC. In smaller LLCs (with fewer owners), ownership is expressed as a percentage and not as a number of units.

NDA. *Nondisclosure agreement* is a one-way or mutual contract between parties who promise not to share protected information outside of a defined circle of need-to-know parties. The tricky part of drafting these is defining the scope of "confidential information." Always work with a lawyer to get that definition right.

nondisclosure agreement. Same as an *NDA*.

nonprofit. Legally, this refers to any entity formed by state law to be a nonprofit under the laws of that state. But colloquially, people use the term to refer to entities that have met the qualifications of the Internal Revenue Code to be a tax-exempt or charitable entity, such as a 501(c)(3) or 501(c)(4).

officer. A specific person appointed to carry out an executive function for a company. The C-suite or senior officers are generally appointed by and report to the board of directors in a corporation or the manager(s) in an LLC. More junior officers will be appointed by other officers. By law, all corporations must have a president, secretary, and treasurer. By common practice, most companies with investors and more than one layer of leadership officially elect people to these positions and often include vice presidents and assistant secretaries and assistant treasurers in the list as backup positions for official actions.

operating agreement. The governing document of a limited liability company. It is the same as a company agreement. Different states (and different lawyers) use different terms for the same document.

open-source license. See *copyrights*.

partner. The owners of a partnership whose rights are defined by the partnership agreement of the partnership.

partnership. There are two kinds of partnerships: general partnerships and limited partnerships.

patent. A special legal protection obtained in the US by successfully filing and receiving and award from the USPTO. See Chapter 10.

private equity. Investors who are putting a bit more money in than angels and probably want more proof of concept. This term can also be used to refer to a private equity or PE fund.

private offering. The offering of the sale of equity (or the issuance of notes) to raise funds from investors in a private company. Sometimes this term is used interchangeably with *exempt offering*. But not all private offerings qualify for exemptions from registration under the federal and state securities laws. *Do not* undertake a private offering (or exempt offering) without a seasoned lawyer.

pro forma Cap Table. The Cap Table of a company prepared in anticipation of the issuance of new equity. It is prepared as if the new equity had already been issued to show what the new ownership percentages are after the new issuance.

proof of concept. See *goals*.

put. The right to require someone to buy an ownership interest.

registered mark. The trademark, tradename, or copyright that has been filed and granted protection as well as the right to use the symbol ®.

S corporation. A corporation that elects to be taxed as a pass-through entity under the special rules set out in Subchapter S of the Internal Revenue Code.

share. A specific unit of ownership in a corporation. Corporations that have raised money with preferred rights or returns have multiple classes of shares.

series A. The first round of equity raised by a corporation *after* the common or founders' round. In certain industries, there can be expectations placed by the private equity or venture fund investors on the rights of series A. But these are always negotiable. Note that in LLCs, it is common to have a new *class* of units instead of using the term *series*.

series B. The second round of equity raised by a corporation after the series A round. In certain industries, there can be expectations placed by the private equity or venture fund investors on the rights of series B. But these are always negotiable.

series LLC. A special form of affiliated group of LLCs with common ownership. It is a bit like a cloning structure where the founders adopt a common form of company agreement and rules to govern a collection of very similar investment entities. It is sometimes used in cookie-cutter real estate transactions where a group of investors is buying several properties and wants to hold each in a separate but identical legal entity. These are relatively new. And they are not fully tested for liability protection purposes yet.

series partnership. Just like series LLC but using a limited partnership structure instead of LLCs.

shareholder. By statute, the owners of a corporation are called shareholders. Their rights are defined by the bylaws and the certificate of formation and under the statute of their state of formation.

sharing ratio or **membership interest percentage.** An LLC member's economic percentage out of the whole ownership.

stock registry. The official roster of shareholders and their shares and the certificate numbers associated with the shares. Corporate law requires that the corporation keep an updated stock registry with the books and records of the company.

trademark. The formal protection of a name, logo, phrase, brand, or similar defining mark that is grated by successfully filing and receiving an award from the USPTO.

tradename. Like a trademark but for names only.

UCC. See *common contract clauses*.

unit. Refers to the membership interest or partnership interest denominated as a specific number instead of a percentage in an LLC. It is a type of equity somewhat equivalent to a share of a corporation.

USPTO. The United States Patent & Trade Office.

value of an equity interest. The value of an owner's specific interest in the company, which may or may not be a function of the value of the company, as discussed in Chapter 12.

venture capital. This commonly refers to investors who are specialized and private (but sometimes corporate), having money to place into a defined type of transaction. Venture capital will form funds with very targeted investment theses.

warranty of fitness for purpose. See *common contract clauses*.

501(c)(3). A form of nonprofit that has been certified by the IRS to be a charity worthy of special tax-exempt status. Generally, the activities are either religious, charitable, or educational, as such categories are specifically defined in Section 501(c)(3) of the Internal Revenue Code.

501(c)(4). Another form of nonprofit certified by the IRS. The activities of these entities are more broadly social welfare activities and can include certain kinds of lobbying and political activism.

HOMEWORK

Chapter 1 Homework

Pizza Party Prep Exercises and Decision Matrices

Pizza Party 1

Prep Exercise 1

Company Visions and Goals

Ask each person invited to the Founders' Table to share their vision, goals, and fears about the new company.

Go around the table and answer these questions. Work on your listening skills. Designate someone to take notes.	
What is the purpose of this company?	
What market niche does it fill?	
Why are we here?	
What do I think I contribute?	
What do I think others contribute?	
Who is missing from this group? What skill sets do we need but don't have?	

What is the endgame for the company from my perspective?	
What is my timeline for participation?	
What is the company's longest imaginable time-line to success?	

Come up with consensus answers around these questions.	
What is the purpose of this company?	
What market niche does it fill?	
Why are we here?	
What does each person at the table contribute? (You will refine this later.)	
Who is missing from this group? What skill sets do we need but don't have?	
What is the endgame for the company from my perspective?	
What is our longest imaginable timeline to success?	
What is my timeline for participation?	
What is the company's longest imaginable time-line to success?	

Good work! You have begun to build your goals and ninety-day timeline as well as starting to understand the Human Factors.

Circulate the consensus answers. Schedule the next Pizza Party.

Pizza Party 2

Prep Exercise 1

Founders' Homework: Who Am I?

Basics	
Name:	
Hometown:	
Key personal relationships:	
Important personal obligations:	
Current job:	
Favorite Ice-cream flavor:	
How do you know the founder?	
Key passions outside of work:	
Who or what are your personal safety nets outside of this group?	
Why are you here?	
What do you think you could/would sacrifice to join this team?	

Why is the sacrifice worth it?	
Could you imagine success?	

Personal Limiting Factors and Role Definition	
When will you run out of patience?	
When will you run out of time?	
When will you run out of behind-the-scenes support?	
What is your hidden baggage?	
Do you have any fear going into this project?	
What do you think you bring to the mix?	
What do you think the group is missing in terms of talents or skills or personalities?	
What role would you be willing to do even if it stretched you personally?	

Pizza Party 2

Prep Exercise 2

What Are the Founders' Roles?

After listening hard to the answers shared in Prep Exercise 1, for each identified founder, answer the following questions. Discuss as a group. Revise answers and then move to the additional prep exercises.

Name:	
Primary skill/value added:	
Role in leadership:	
How long can you commit?	
What are your outside commitments?	
Who do you report to in the founder group?	
Who reports to you?	
Do you trust each member?	
What do you need to tell the founders that might be hidden baggage?	
What do you need to know from the founders that might be hidden baggage?	
Do you have a significant other who is supporting or resisting in this venture?	

Pizza Party 2

Prep Exercise 3

Who Are We as a Group?

Personalities and Talents—Balance in Leadership	
Is there a good balance of vision and execution?	
Do you have at least one peacemaker?	
Does everyone have a support system outside the group?	
Are there any toxic behaviors or personalities?	
Are there any people who have limitations?	
Do you understand everyone's motivations and expectations?	

Prep Exercise 4

Wearing the Right Hats

Do We Have the Right Roles Identified?

Remember that each person at the table likely is already wearing the hats of equity owner, visionary, and leader in some way or another.

Now you need to drill deeper into the concrete roles required to get the job done—to execute on your business plan, raise capital, market, build, and operate the business. This is another collection of hats or roles.

At a minimum, each company needs a solid leadership player who understands:

- finance
- people dynamics
- vision and direction
- technology
- operations
- marketing

Tech companies need specialized leaders who understand development, privacy, hardware, software, and the legal landscape.

A construction company will require someone who clearly understands permitting and planning. A bakery needs a baker.

Do We Have the Right Players Wearing the Right Hats?

Role:	Player(s):
Finance	
People dynamics	
Vision and direction	
Technology	
Operations	
Marketing	

Do two or more people fill the same roles?

Are there any vacancies or missing skill sets?

What additional roles need to be filled by founders or by others?

Role:	Player(s):
Investor relations	
Asset management	
Logistics	
Regulatory compliance	
Legal	
Other:	
Other:	
Other:	

Bonus Points: Other Human Factors	
Who is not at the table and should be?	
Who is not at the table but seems to be whispering in?	
Have we considered everyone's past failures and what they learned?	

Do we have any outsized egos that might shift balances of power?	
Do our leadership paradigm and business plan consider personal, behind-the-scenes issues identified in the founders' homework?	

Pizza Party 3

Identify Your Leadership Paradigm

Now that you have identified the founders, you need to identify which leadership paradigm fits your group. Refer to the descriptions below and choose what seems to suit the existing dynamics of the group most. Keep in mind that this will likely change over time—and it should change over time. But it is valuable to choose a model to start your journey and create governance rules consistent with the founders' expectations in the context of the model.

Review the following models and decide which fits your vision right now, in twelve months, and in twenty-four months.

Enlightened dictatorship	This is most common when there is a strong personality at the helm who has come up with the *great idea*, done some of the funding, assembled the team, and been the primary driving force to this point. The author of a book is its enlightened dictator. What other examples come to mind? This can be a very stable and successful initial leadership model if all founders and others consent to it and if the boundaries are clearly stated from the outset. Some companies exist as enlightened dictatorships all the way to an exit or to a generational change.
Oligarchy	A small group of equal leaders. This model is less stable over the long term than an enlightened dictatorship simply because it depends on a small group (three to five people at most) aligning their interests, energy, economics, and passions for an extended period. Service companies such as accounting firms, doctors' offices, law firms, architects, and so on often start as oligarchies. So do younger founders who are launching businesses at a period in their lives when all members of the group have discretionary time and energy to commit to the new deal. To make this work, the oligarchy will need to build a great deal of trust and will need to focus carefully on the *Decision Matrix*.
Democracy	This is the default model if there is not a single strong leader and there are more people in the founders' group than can reasonably function as an oligarchy. It is rarely stable for companies or countries over long periods of stressful and unpredictable growth. Service companies often start this way yet slip quickly but informally into dictatorships or oligarchies, without thinking through minority protection rights.

Representative democracy	This is the classic corporate model and is most common and most stable for mature enterprises with fiscal and directional stability. A corporation consists of shareholders/investors who are generally passive, reserving the right to vote by selling their interests or by electing directors. The directors represent the investor/money interest and provide big-picture and directional guidance (hence the word *director*). Directors, in turn, elect officers to run the day-to-day business. It is rare for this model to work in classic corporate form for start-up or evolving companies. But variations on the theme are endless—and a good lawyer can help you work through how to balance interests and talents in this format.
Fifty/fifty	*Warning*: This is the least stable and most dangerous leadership model. Two, four, or even six individuals rarely see eye to eye for extended periods through growth, stress, change, and evolution in the business and personal lives. Deadlock is common and very difficult. There are some short-term ways to create a bridge between the fifty/fifty structure and a more stable model. But always beware that the devil of deadlock looms in the background.

Now that you have learned about the five leadership paradigms, answer the following questions:

What type of leadership paradigm does the company currently have?	
What type of leadership paradigm do you prefer for the company?	
What type of leadership paradigm do your investors prefer for the company?	
Can the company start with one leadership paradigm and evolve into another?	

Chapter 1

Decision Matrix Examples

Decision Matrix 1

Real Estate Development—Fifty/Fifty Owners

Decision	Owner 1	Owner 2	Both	Tiebreak Option (or Advisory Board Decisions)
Select Property for Development			X	Don't do the deal
Negotiate Financing	X			
Select Architect and Approve Plans		X		
Manage GC and Project Flow		X		
Insurance, Accounting, Legal Services		X		
Develop Marketing Plan	X			
Approve and Negotiate Sales	X			
Tax Compliance	X			
Capital Calls	X	X	X	Usually, one partner will have the right to buy out the other if one won't or can't fund

Decision Matrix 2

Accounting, Law, Architecture, Designer, Other Services—Fifty/Fifty Owners

Decision	Owner 1	Owner 2	Both	Tiebreak Option
Select Name			X	Don't do the deal
Negotiate Lease	X			
Manage Legal Formation		X		
Establish House Rules for Client Engagements			X	Bring in an adviser
Insurance, Accounting, Legal Services		X		
Develop Marketing Plan	X			
Hiring and Firing other Professionals		X		Don't take action
Hiring and Firing Support Staff	X	X		
Admitting New Partners			X	Don't take action
Tax Compliance	X			
Capital Calls	X	X	X	May need to divorce if the venture needs funds and the parties can't agree

Decision Matrix 3

Software Company—Enlightened Dictatorship

Decision	Lead Founder/ Manager	Board Majority	Owner Majority	Notes
Original Business Plan	X	X	X	Don't do the deal
Negotiate Financing or Equity Raise	X	X		
Capital Calls	X	X		
Design Decision	X			
Manage Project Flow	X			
Insurance, Accounting, Legal Services		X		
Develop Marketing Plan	X			
Approve and Negotiate Sales	X			
Tax Compliance	X			
Hiring and Firing	X			
Budget	X			
Approve Big Contracts	X			
Sign a Lease	X			
Approve Software Development Team and Process	X			

Approve Strategic Alliances	X	X		
Approve Sale of Company	X	X	X	
Remove the Enlightened Dictator		X	X	Probably have to show cause or negotiate a painful buyout

Decision Matrix 4

Consumer Business—Representative Democracy

Decision	President	Board Majority	Members by Majority	Tiebreak Option
Original Business Plan	X	X	X	Don't do the deal
Negotiate Financing or Equity Raise	X	X	X	
Capital Calls	X	X	X	
Final Design Decision	X	X		
Manage Project Flow	X			
Insurance, Accounting, Legal Services	X			
Oversee Accounting	X			
Approve Marketing Plan	X	X		
Approve and Negotiate Sales	X			
Tax Compliance	X			
Appoint Officers and Define Duties	X	X		
Hiring and Firing	X			
Budget	X	X		

Approve Big Contracts	X	X		
Approve Strategic Alliances	X	X		
Approve a Sale of Company	X	X	X	

Decision Matrix 5

Your Turn! Company Leadership Paradigm:

Decision				Notes

Chapter 2 Homework

Finding the Money Now

1. Fill in the chart below with all founders.
2. Call your lawyer.
3. Call your banker.
4. Call your accountant.
5. Call your FFFs.
6. Finalize a plan.

	Who Can help you figure it out?	What outsiders might help you?	What legal processes are required before you can take the money and run?
How much money do you need today?			
Who has the money you need?			
What do they want in exchange?			
Can you borrow funds?			
Are you eligible for any grants or special subsidies?			
Do you know the value of the company?			

Chapter 3 Homework

Micro and Macro Goals; Ninety-Day Timeline

Goal Worksheet

What is your macro goal?	
Why?	

	Pros	Cons
Sell Out Soon		

	Pros	Cons
Build and Hold		

Note that your investors will all need to understand these macro goals clearly and will ask you about them frequently.

Now you can establish some micro goals. I recommend that you think about people and product and market and money each quarter:

First Quarter	
People Goals	
Product Goals	
Market Goals	
Money Goals	

Second Quarter	
People Goals	
Product Goals	
Market Goals	
Money Goals	

Third Quarter	
People Goals	
Product Goals	
Market Goals	
Money Goals	

Fourth Quarter	
People Goals	
Product Goals	
Market Goals	
Money Goals	

Ninety-Day Timeline

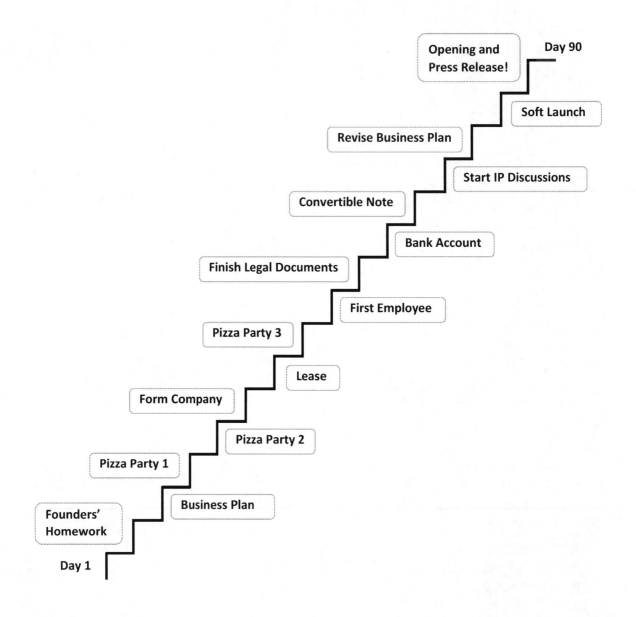

Day 90

Opening and
Press Release!

Soft Launch

Revise Business Plan

Start IP Discussions

Convertible Note

Bank Account

Finish Legal Documents

First Employee

Pizza Party 3

Lease

Form Company

Pizza Party 2

Pizza Party 1

Business Plan

Founders'
Homework

Day 1

More Details for Ninety-Day Timeline

- Great idea.
- Bounce off FFFs (friends, fools, and family).
- Prepare a timeline.
- Prepare a budget for your first six months.
- Work on your team—chapters 1 and 2.
- Hire a lawyer.
- Form a legal entity with founders.
- Raise seed capital.
- Do your homework on IP issues.
- Do your homework on government and regulatory issues.
- Revise your budget.
- Raise more money.
- Revise your timeline.
- Add more players to your team (go through chapter 1 again).
- Begin putting money into product/capital.
- Sign a lease.
- License required rights (lawyer required).
- Make sure you understand employees versus independent contractors and have your staff set up properly.
- Engage an outsourced payroll company.
- Find an accountant and adopt a real bookkeeping system.
- Circle back with your lawyer about the legal issues around raising money.
- Pitch to investors.
- Raise more money or close your first raise.
- Do your homework on your competition. No—*really do your homework.*
- Make your list of prospective customers and make a plan for courting them.
- Put a PR plan in place.
- Revisit your team dynamics (chapter 1).
- Add to your team or change out team members.
- Create a new ninety-day plan.

Chapter 4 Homework

Choice of Entity

Use this helpful homework game to assist your decision when it comes to the choice of entity. For each question, choose *yes* or *no*. Then add the designated amount of point along with the type of entity to the entity box. Calculate your score at the end to determine what type of entity best suits your company.

Tax Questions	LLC	Corp	Y/N
Will the company have losses in the first few tax years? (Yes = 1 point for LLC)			
Will the company mostly have private investors? (Yes = 2 points for LLC)			
Will the company need to raise additional funds? (Yes = 2 points for LLC)			
Does the company need or want a 401(k)? (Yes = 2 points for Corporation)			
Are there any entity investors? (Yes = S Corp is not allowed [some exceptions])			
Are you taking on substantial related party debt that can't later be capitalized? (Yes = 2 points for corporation)			

Management Questions	LLC	Corp	Y/N
Do you need a formal board of directors or do your investors demand one? (Yes = 2 points for corporation)			
Is your management style still evolving? (Yes = 2 points for LLC)			
Are you in the enlightened dictator phase? (Yes = 2 points for LLC)			
Are you a fifty/fifty venture? (Yes = 2 points for corporation)			

Are there any entity investors? (Yes = S Corp is not allowed [some exceptions])			
Do your investors have a strong preference for a corporation?			
Add up your points to calculate your score			

Most early-stage companies will find LLCs fit their start-up needs best. There are exceptions. And tax laws change frequently. Check with your tax adviser *and* your corporate lawyer before you decide on the right form of entity. Sometimes it makes sense to form two entities to accomplish your goals. This is not a simple decision. But you can also change your course later as your needs evolve.

New Company Document Checklist

Document	Executed By	Filed	Outside Adviser
Certificate of Formation			
Decision Matrix (See Chapter 1)			
Company/Operating Agreement (LLCS)			
Bylaws (Corp)			
Shareholder's Agreement (Corp and Addendum to Company Agreement)			
Organizational Meeting Minutes (Corp)			
FEIN from IRS			
Independent Contractor Agreement			
Form of Offer letter for Employees			
Employee Policies			

Licenses or Assignment of Rights for all SAS or Software or IP Used			
Management/Employment Services Agreement			
Convertible Note Form?			

Chapter 5 Homework

B Corp, Nonprofit, or LLC

	B Corp	Nonprofit	LLC with Special Purpose Clauses
Do you want to make money for yourself?	Yes	Only in reasonable salary	Yes
Do your investors *need* to make money?	Yes, but subject to special B purposes	No	Yes
Is your money coming from a small, defined group that wants to control the outcomes?	B Corp	Nonprofit	Yes
Are you supporting another existing charity with profits instead of directly doing charity work?	Yes	Possibly— could become a supporting organization	Yes
Are you involving the broader community in benefits and also in influencing direction?	Yes	Yes	Yes
Does your principal business involve selling something, making something for wholesale, leasing something, or providing services?	Yes	No	Yes
Are you a religion, educational institution, or political supporting organization, working with economic needs and community needs?	Yes	Yes	Yes

Chapter 6 Homework

Lease Checklist and Distribution Agreement Checklist

You have probably already signed at least one lease in your life by the time you read this book. But it is likely that you signed a residential lease for an apartment or house. Residential leases are subject to tenant protections set out in state and local law. Commercial leases are not. Commercial landlords are, by nature, aggressive, overreaching, and very unbalanced in drafting their contracts. If you just sign what you are given, you may end up with huge hidden risks and no real way to get out of the contract or force the landlord to make it right.

> **Story**. Hurricane Harvey devastated the city of Houston. Water from the flooded bayous poured into basements and even ground-level and first floors of major office buildings. Roofs caved in, and elevator shafts filled with water. HVAC systems died. In short, the buildings became unusable—not just for a week or two but for years. Tenants are still suing landlords to try to get out of leases, force the landlords to re-mediate damage, and recover some funds. Those tenants who signed the form leases provided by the commercial building managers are having a very, very tough time recovering anything, and some have filed for bankruptcy. Those who negotiated some key protective terms have moved on with their lives.

A. Standard Revisions. Standard revisions made to nearly every commercial lease:

1. **Notice addresses**: Accurate notice addressees for tenant (including addresses for before and after the commencement date, if needed), including a copy to tenant's leasing counsel.
2. **Landlord's consent**: Not to be unreasonably withheld, conditioned, or delayed wherever encountered, but especially as to assignments and subleases.
3. **As is**: Exclude latent defects, hazardous materials. and work required to be done by landlord.
4. **Commencement date**: Clarify/correct definition to protect tenant.
5. **Leasehold improvements**: Clarify/correct landlord's work, tenant's work, and so on. (Note: any work not specifically included in landlord's work will likely become tenant's responsibility.)
6. **ADA**: Clarify/correct the parties' respective responsibilities (if applicable). (Note: any ADA work not specifically required to be performed by landlord could become tenant's responsibility.)

7. **Security deposit**: Clarify/correct provisions re security deposit, including landlord's obligation to provide a detailed accounting of any portion not returned by landlord.

8. **Rules and regulations**: Should be enforced in a nondiscriminatory manner.

9. **Maintenance and repairs**. Clarify each party's maintenance obligations. (Note: any work not specifically required to be performed by landlord could become tenant's responsibility.)

10. **Landlord's right of entry**: Bolster limitations on landlord's right to enter the premises, such as prior notice except in emergencies; accompanied by an agent of tenant; minimizing interference; work to be performed after hours; controlled access to secure areas; and so on.

11. **Parking**: Clarify/correct parking rights and areas. Quite variable, depending on facilities.

12. **Service interruptions**: Clarify/correct tenant's rights, including landlord's negligence, rent abatement, and termination.

13. **Insurance**: Clarify/correct insurance provisions, including tenant and landlord requirements; blanket policies; waiver of subrogation; and so on. The insurance and indemnity provisions should be reviewed by tenant's risk manager.

14. **Indemnities**: Make indemnities mutual. Resist "express negligence" provisions.

15. **Casualty and condemnation**: Clarify/correct provisions regarding notice of reconstruction period; both parties' termination rights; rent abatement following event and during reconstruction; damage to common areas; right to proceeds and awards; and so on.

16. **Assignment and subleasing**: Add protections, such as landlord's consent deemed given if no response within fifteen days; original tenant's liability not continuing into subsequent renewal periods with assignee; splitting upside rent fifty/fifty after deducting expenses; and consent not required for assignment in connection with merger, consolidation, reorganization, or sale of substantially all assets or stock.

17. **Defaults and remedies**: Add protections, such as five days' written notice; extendable non-monetary default cure periods; duty to mitigate with specific actions required; landlord's default; and so on.

18. **Limitations on landlord's liability**: Clarify landlord's "interest in the project" to include rents and sale proceeds.

19. **Consequential and special damages**: Add mutual waiver.

20. **Surrender**: Clarify/correct provisions re surrender of premises, including disavowing any obligation by tenant to remove leasehold improvements.

21. **Holdover**: Reduce rent multiplier factor and resist indemnity for lost deals.

22. **Hazardous materials**: Landlord reps no knowledge; tenant disclaimer for preexisting HazMat or any caused by anyone other than tenant; and right to terminate for extended contamination event not caused by tenant. Who handles asbestos removal if required?

23. **Force Majeure (Acts of God)**: Add or make mutual; and add pandemics.

24. **Brokers**: Clarify/correct provisions, mutual indemnity, and commissions payable by landlord pursuant to separate agreements.

25. **Attorneys' fees**: Clarify/correct provisions re attorneys' fees, making mutual based on prevailing party.

26. **Governing law; venue**: Should be in county and state where the property is located.

27. **OFAC**: Make mutual and add where missing.

28. **Conditions precedent**: Add landlord representations re clear title and compliance with laws.

B. CUSTOM PROVISIONS. Provisions typically customized to each deal:

1. **Delayed delivery of premises**: Tenant may need to terminate if landlord fails to deliver the premises in the required condition by a specified "outside date" through no fault of tenant.
2. **Early access**: Tenant usually needs early access to the premises for inspection, measurements, photos, space planning, monitoring work progress, installing FF&E, and so on.
3. **Building permits**: Tenant may need an outside date by which the building permit must be issued, whether being obtained by landlord or tenant.
4. **Operating expenses:**
    (a) annual cap on "controllable" operating expenses
    (b) grossing up only applies to occupancy-related expenses
    (c) cap on management fees (3 percent)
    (d) exclusions from operating expenses and taxes—full bore or basics?
    (e) audit rights?
5. **Related users**: Will any independent contractors or other nonemployees be routinely occupying and using space in the premises?
6. **Tenant self-help**: Does tenant need the right to make repairs if landlord fails to do so after written notice or in emergencies? Usually not appropriate in multitenant office or retail leases; more appropriate in single-tenant facilities.
7. **Utilities**: Premises already metered for utilities? If not, who is responsible for installing them?
8. **Signs**: Any building, door, monument. or pylon signage rights? If so, get preapproval of tenant's standard signage package and attach as a lease exhibit.
9. **SNDA**: Does landlord have a loan on the project? If so, does tenant need a subordination, nondisturbance, and attornment agreement from landlord's lender?
10. **Landlord's lien exclusions**: Will tenant need any purchase money or leasehold financing?
11. **HVAC:**
    (a) Existing or new rooftop units? If new, who installs and at whose expenses?
    (b) If existing, ask for an inspection report and a warranty from landlord (twelve to twenty-four months).
12. **Guaranty**: Seek limitations, such as base rent only, initial or shorter term, burn-off, money caps, and so on.

C. Special Retail Provisions

1. **Exclusive**: Does tenant need an exclusive to protect its business?
2. **Percentage rent**: Exclusions from "gross sales."
3. **Continuous operations / go-dark clause (retail only):**
    (a) Is tenant willing to covenant to continuously operate its business in the premises?
    (b) Does tenant need the right to close shop for an extended period (60, 90, 180 days)?
4. **No build zone**: Does tenant need to block off area to ensure visibility to main road?

Note: This checklist is not a comprehensive catalog of all potential issues a tenant may encounter in a commercial lease submitted by a prospective landlord; rather, this is an overview of the most common issues a tenant will likely face. It should be clear from the foregoing checklist that leasing is far more complex and fraught with risk than most people think. Moreover, the issues raised above are stated in shorthand fashion, which will not suffice in a formal legal lease agreement. Finally, every lease transaction is different in certain ways from other deals, however similar they may seem. The facts on the ground matter greatly. For these reasons and more, please retain an experienced leasing attorney to assist you in reviewing, understanding, and negotiating your commercial lease.

Distribution Agreement Checklist

D.   Key Elements of Independent Distribution Agreement

E.   (Pro Distributor)

1. **Definition of product** (exactly what are you authorized to sell)
2. **Definition of target market/buyers**: Are there specific targeted customers (e.g., State of Texas, first responders, US Coast Guard, St. Luke's Hospital System)?
3. **Are there any excluded markets in the territory**? (e.g., reserved to other distributors)
4. **Definition of territory**: regional, national, or multinational
5. **Definition of exclusivity**: per product, territory, or target buyers
6. **Term**: How long does the contract last?
7. **Who can terminate it**?
    a.   Why/when/how?
8. **What commissions does distributor receive**?
    a.   percent of gross
    b.   fee per item
9. **Warranties**: The company warrants that company products will conform to published specifications and be free from defects in material or workmanship for a period of one year from the date of delivery or for the period of the company's standard warranty for company products, whichever is greater.
10. **What samples or product demo/marketing material are paid for and authorized by seller**? (Will you receive a kit with samples, demos, product promotional materials, etc.?)
11. **Is the distributor required to attend certain conventions, demos, or events**?
    a.   Who covers the cost of attendance?
12. **Are you allowed to set up your own website and social media presence**?
13. **Can you rep other noncompetitive products**?
    a.   Can you rep competitive products?
14. **Does distributor have any minimum sales requirements**?
    a.   Over what period of time?
    b.   Is this reasonable in the marketplace?
15. **What sales terms does seller promise**?
    a.   price
    b.   delivery
    c.   quality
    d.   warranty
    e.   special qualifications, like medical certifications etc.
16. **Can seller compete in the same market**?
17. **Can seller agree to change terms for one prospective buyer but not for others**?
18. **Is distributor allowed to offer "most favored nations" terms**?
19. **Contract should have complete and explicit antibribery terms applicable to both seller and distributor.**
20. **Who owns the seller**? OFAC rules, anti–money laundering rules

21. **Can the materials be legally imported?**
22. **Indemnification of distributor for damages directly or indirectly arising out of:**
    a.   material breach by seller of distribution agreement or any PO or sales agreement
    b.   misrepresentation by seller
    c.   named in a lawsuit by a buyer for any reason other than malfeasance, material misconduct, or fraud by distributor
    d.   breach of NDA
    e.   breach by seller of exclusivity arrangements
23. **Stand-alone or integrated NDA—recommend term of agreement plus one year.**
24. **Optional**
    a.   nonsolicit
    b.   no hire

Chapter 7 Homework

Defining the Deal

Each time you enter into *any* kind of contract, get in the habit of filling in this checklist. This process, when it becomes a habit, will prevent you from entering into handshake transactions with ambiguous terms.

Who is buying?		
Who is selling?		
Is it a sale of goods or services or both?		
Is it recurring or a one-time deal?		
Describe the products or services in a way that a dumb lawyer can understand.		
Is the supplier dependent on outside factors (like another supplier, the weather, financing, etc.) in order to complete the order?		
Is the deal an "exclusive" or "requirements" deal?		

What are all of the terrible, horrible, very bad things that could go wrong?		
What risk-management terms are in the contract in case all of the very bad things happen?		

Chapter 8 Homework

Green, Yellow, Red Homework

Sort your Key Contributors into three groups: green, yellow, and red.

Name and Title	Job Description	How Are They Paid? (Hourly, Salary, Equity?)	Long-Term or Short-Term Tour of Duty	Green, Yellow, or Red?

Green: Independent contractors and short-term service employees.

Yellow: Long-term key players contributing core services or ideas. May include some officers.

Red: Core contributors who might see themselves as founders. Expects some kind of equity or equity-like bonus plan.

Employee versus Independent Contractor Worksheet

	Yes	No	Net?
Service provider is an entity rather than an individual.	+ 1	-1	
If an entity, service provider has other employees?	+ 1	-1	
More than three other employees?	+ 1	0	
Service provider has other customers?	+ 2	-1	
Is service provider a full-time student?	+1	-1	
Service provider provides own materials/equipment?	+ 1	-1	
Company allows service provider to work any hours-of-service provider's choosing?	+ 2	-2	
Service provider has a sleeping bag in company's office and works long hours?	-4	+1	
Service provider is permitted to work at home or at location of his/her choosing (i.e., not required to be in contracting attorney's office)? (Less important since COVID.)	+ 1	-1	
Contracting attorney is concerned only about the result of service provider's work and does not direct the manner in which the work is carried out?	+1	-1	
Service provider is sophisticated enough to pay its own quarterly tax estimates?	+ 1	-1	
Service provider receives payment by the job done / hours worked, not fixed payments on a regular basis?	+ 1	-1	
Service provider has his/her own health insurance?	+ 1	-1	
Contracting attorney does not need to provide substantial training to service provider?	+ 1	-1	
Is it a fixed and short-term engagement (e.g., summer months)?	+1	-1	
Service provider can do his/her work without the presence of contracting attorney or others on contracting attorney's team?	+1	-1	
Service provider has never brought an employment-related lawsuit or other type of claim against anyone in the past?	+1	-3	
Total?			

If your score is not at least 12, you may have inadvertently created an employment relationship.

If you answered no to anything in *italics*, even if your score was 14, you may have the appearance of an employment relationship.

Each state and the IRS have their own rules and their own way of interpreting the rules. So, you need to consult with local counsel before paying someone as an independent contractor.

Chapter 9 Homework

Regulatory Word on the Street

Do a comprehensive online search on your prospective competitors and industry trends.

	Notes
Are there lawsuits by competitors, employees, or customers that allege breach of regulations or appearance of breach of public policy?	
Are there big public social media controversies about your competitors? Do they revolve around actual or perceived violations of government or public policies?	
Try searching in local newspapers instead of just doing a general search online. Specialized business journals, like the *Houston Business Journal*, often dive deep into regionally important regulatory issues.	
Dig into the key words like "consumer protection" if you are opening a direct-to-consumer business.	
What did you learn about the hazards in your business that you didn't know before?	

Bonus points if you join a local trade association, attend a community college class targeting your industry, or put a seasoned veteran of your business on your advisory board.	
Network and learn from the mistakes of others. It is easy to have your head in the sand as you build your idea into an enterprise.	

Chapter 10 Homework

IP (Patents and Trademarks)

First, you need to decide what to patent. Then you need to evaluate whether it is worth it. Fill out this chart and review it carefully with your strategic team, including your designers, engineers, marketing team, finance group, and outside advisers before developing a budget and timeline for any patent.

Question	Answer	Notes
Is there a "special sauce" that gives your innovation a marketplace advantage, and if so, is it something that you can protect by patent?		
What feature or combination of features is/are required to compete with you effectively (and constitute your Strait of Hormuz)?		
Is patent protection barred for any reason?		Common roadblock: the product has been on sale for more than a year.
What is the income source for your products/services, and is it tied to your special sauce?		
How long is the product cycle for your products/services (more protection for longer product cycles)?		

Question	Answer	Notes
What is your target market(s)?		
Is broad protection available?		Are you sure there is nothing like your product in the marketplace?
Will a patent provide higher margins?		If no one could copy the product, could you demand a higher price?
Does the invention have strategic value?		Can others compete effectively without your innovation?
Is there licensing potential to the product?		
Is filing necessary to preserve foreign rights?		If you do not file before first sale, foreign rights will be lost forever.
Is there a contractual obligation to file?		Your investors or major customers may have required this.
Is invention consistent with your strategic business objectives?		It will be expensive. Do you really need it?

Chapter 11 Homework

Buy-Sell Checklist

Buy-Sell Agreement Trigger Events	Buyout (Y/N)	Comments
Disappears/quits		
Disappears/retires		
Disabled short-term		
Disabled long-term		
Dies		
Divorced		
Default (bankruptcy)		
Disqualification		
Disagreement		
Dispute resolution		

Other Situations That May Warrant Consideration	Allowed (Y/N)	Comments
Rights of first refusal to other owners		
Secondary right of refusal to company		
Optional purchase/sale		
Mandatory purchase		
Life insurance		
Maintenance of S corporation status		
Control maintenance		
Vote restrictions or agreements		
Personal guarantees		

Pricing Methods			Comments
Fixed price	Price per agreement?	$	
	Date of price?	/ /	
	Alternative(s) if price is out of date? (Is there a valuation process in the event that the fixed price is dated?) Then, it is also a process agreement and must be evaluated as such.	Yes / No	
Third-party man-date price	Is there a third-party reference price (broker/dealer, reinsurer, etc.)?	Yes / No	
Formula	Does agreement specify who to calculate?	Yes / No	
	If so, who?	Notes	
	Date of last calculation?	/ /	
	Price per last calculation?	$	
Valuation process with appraiser(s)	Type of process? *		
	Appraiser(s) named in agreement?	Yes / No	
	If so, who?	Notes	
	Has the process ever been triggered?	Yes / No	
	If yes, when?	/ /	

Life Insurance	
Amount(s)	Corporate / Individual Owners
$	
$	
$	
$	

Printed in the United States
by Baker & Taylor Publisher Services